THE ENCOURAGEMENT FACTOR

Give Me One More Inch

Dedication

I would first like to start off by thanking my Lord and Savior, Jesus Christ, for allowing me to live long enough to author this book, and for giving me the gift of encouragement and empowerment. I would also like to thank Him for my family that He blessed me with. My mom, Nellie Barnett, who modeled hard-work, love, and sacrifice. My wife, who has been with me through thick and thin. Thank you, Cassandra, for always believing in me and encouraging me to continue to press on, despite how things may look on the outside. My girls, Precious and Morgan, who have continually challenged and encouraged me to invest in myself the same way I invest in others. My boys, Xavier and Simeon, who have been there to encourage me and push me forward when I didn't think what I was doing mattered. I would also like to thank my grandkids for inspiring and encouraging me to leave the world better for their generation.

I would like to thank all my other family members, friends, teachers, coaches, pastors, bosses, and associates, who allowed me to share my gift of encouragement with them.

A special thanks to Morgan for her special contributions, Simeon for encouraging me to meet a deadline, and Bradley Watson for his photography assistance, book layout, and cover design.

Table of Contents

I can't begin to explain how exciting it is to finally be publishing this book. It's a milestone I've talked about for years. I finally took my own advice, as well as the encouragement of my family and friends and did it. Enjoy!

The original title for this book was *The 5 Essentials of Empowerment* and it was based on a list of essentials that pave the journey of empowerment. As I begun the writing process, I realized that it would be more effective if I narrowed my focus to just one of the essentials. Deciding which one to initially focus on was a challenging task. I ultimately settled on **encouragement**. Encouragement is a crucial need in today's culture because it motivates people, boosts mental well-being, strengthens relationships, empowers individuals, and creates a positive atmosphere. By offering genuine support and affirmation, we can make a significant difference in people's lives and contribute to a more uplifting society.

Let me also share why I chose the title and subtitle: "The Encouragement Factor: Give Me One More Inch".

The Encouragement Factor is a concept that emphasizes the power of positive reinforcement and support in motivating individuals to achieve their goals and overcome challenges. It recognizes that a little encouragement can go a long way in boosting confidence, resilience, and determination.

The phrase "Give me one more inch" is often used in motivational and self-improvement contexts to encourage individuals to push themselves a little further, even when they feel like giving up or when success seems out of reach. It signifies the importance of perseverance and the belief that small steps forward can eventually lead to considerable progress.

By adopting the Encouragement Factor and embracing the "Give me one more inch" mindset, individuals can cultivate a positive outlook and develop the inner strength needed to overcome obstacles. It's about focusing on one's potential, celebrating small victories, and continuously striving for improvement.

Whether applied to personal goals, professional aspirations, or any other aspect of life, the Encouragement Factor reminds us of the profound impact that support, positivity, and determination can have on our journey towards success.

Even though the focus is on encouragement, please read this section to gain a full understanding of *The 5 Essentials of Empowerment*. The essentials can have a profound impact on shaping a person's life and can greatly influence their trajectory. When combined and applied effectively, they can contribute to personal growth, success, and fulfillment. However, it is essential to note that the way these essentials are applied can vary, and their impact can be positive or negative.

In the context of leadership, understanding and utilizing these essentials is crucial. Effective leaders recognize the importance of motivation, encouragement, support, and empowerment in guiding and inspiring their team members. They create an environment where individuals feel valued, motivated, and empowered to reach their full potential.

On the other hand, misapplication or neglect of these essentials can have detrimental effects. Lack of motivation, discouragement, unsupportive environments, and disempowerment can hinder personal and professional growth. It is important for leaders to be aware of how their actions and behaviors impact others and strive to apply these essentials in a positive and constructive manner.

Through my leadership journey, I have witnessed both the positive and negative effects of applying these essentials. By recognizing their significance and striving to apply them effectively, a leader can make a positive impact on the lives of those they lead, creating an environment conducive to growth, success, and well-being.

When misapplied, they can have a devastating impact. In an era where depression and self-loathing are at an all-time high, I've noticed that most people just need someone to come alongside them for the journey, and as a result, they will soar. Many individuals struggle with feelings of inadequacy, self-doubt, and despair, and a lack of encouragement can exacerbate these negative emotions.

The following pages will provide an explanation for each of the essentials. Even though the book isn't focused on each these essentials, it is greatly beneficial for you to commit them to memory!

These five principles—engage, encourage, education, equipping, and empowerment—form a framework for supporting individuals and helping them achieve their goals. Let's explore each principle in more detail:

1) Engage: Engaging with people means meeting them where they are in terms of their interests, needs, and circumstances. It involves actively listening, understanding their perspectives, and building connections. By engaging with others, you can establish a foundation of trust and rapport, which is essential for effective collaboration and support.

2) Encourage: Encouragement is about instilling belief and confidence in individuals. It means recognizing their potential, goals and vision, providing positive reinforcement and motivation. Encouragement helps people overcome challenges, maintain their focus, and stay committed to their aspirations.

3) Education: Education involves providing knowledge, information, and resources to individuals who may lack the necessary skills or understanding to achieve their goals. It includes teaching practical skills, offering guidance and mentorship, and sharing relevant information. Education empowers people by equipping them with the knowledge they need to succeed.

4) Equipping: Equipping refers to providing individuals with the tools, resources, and support they require to accomplish their objectives. It may involve providing physical resources, such as technology or materials, or offering training and skill development opportunities. Equipping individuals ensures they have the necessary means to effectively pursue their goals.

5) Empowerment: Empowerment involves creating an environment that allows individuals to take action and make decisions autonomously. It means granting individuals the authority, opportunities, and resources to execute their plans and make a positive impact. Empowerment fosters self-confidence, autonomy, and a sense of ownership, enabling individuals to realize their full potential.

By applying these principles—engaging, encouraging, educating, equipping, and empowering—you can provide comprehensive support to individuals, helping them overcome obstacles, develop their abilities, and fulfill their aspirations.

However, before we move on, I feel that I need to explain equipping and empowering a little more.

Even though they are sometimes used interchangeably, you would be correct to understand that equipping and empowering are distinct steps along the journey to empowerment. While they are related and interconnected, they have different focuses and implications.

Let's further differentiate these two:

Equipping involves providing individuals with the necessary tools, resources, and support to carry out a task or achieve their goals. It is about ensuring that individuals have the physical, technical, or informational resources they need to be effective in their work. This can include providing training, technology, materials, or any other resources required for the task at hand. Equipping sets the foundation for success by removing barriers and enabling individuals to perform their work efficiently.

While equipping is a key step in the process, it is not the last step.

Empowering, on the other hand, goes beyond just providing resources and tools. It involves creating an environment that fosters autonomy, decision-making authority, and accountability.

Empowerment focuses on granting individuals the power and freedom to make decisions, take ownership of their work, and have a say in the outcomes. It is about enabling individuals to act independently, take risks, and learn from their experiences. Empowerment encourages individuals to think critically, be innovative, and develop leadership skills.

Leaders should recognize the distinction between equipping and empowering and ensure that both aspects are addressed. While providing the right tools is crucial, it is equally important to foster an empowering environment that encourages individuals to take initiative, make decisions, and grow personally and professionally.

Encouragement plays a crucial role in uplifting individuals and helping them overcome challenges. It can provide a glimmer of hope and instill confidence in their abilities. Often, a simple word of support or acknowledgement can make a significant difference in someone's life. By providing genuine encouragement, we can help individuals regain their self-esteem, reframe their mindset, and find the strength to overcome obstacles.

In a culture where depression and self-loathing are widespread, being a source of encouragement can be transformative. It allows individuals to recognize their worth, realize their potential, and believe in themselves. Encouragement creates a positive ripple effect, inspiring individuals to take action, pursue their goals, and ultimately soar to new heights.

It's important to remember that encouragement should be sincere, empathetic, and tailored to the individual's needs. It involves actively listening, offering constructive feedback, and providing support in a way that resonates with them. By being a beacon of encouragement, you can contribute to combating the prevalent issues of depression and self-loathing and help individuals find the strength to overcome their challenges.

People generally want to succeed and are willing to put in the effort, but they can sometimes feel hopeless and discouraged.

6 Encouragement Strategies To Overcome Discouragement

These strategies are effective ways to help individuals overcome feelings of hopelessness and discouragement and regain motivation. By providing support, empathy, practical assistance, and breaking goals into smaller steps, you can make the journey seem more manageable and less overwhelming.

Here are 6 strategic approaches to encouraging individuals to overcome discouragement and pursue success:

1. Support and Empathy: Show genuine care and understanding for the challenges they are facing. Be a listening ear and provide emotional support. Let them know that they are not alone in their struggles.

2. Practical Assistance: Offer practical help and resources that can aid them in their journey. This could include sharing knowledge, providing guidance, or connecting them with relevant tools or networks.

3. Break Goals into Smaller Steps: Help individuals break down their goals into smaller, achievable tasks. This approach allows them to make progress incrementally and experience a sense of accomplishment along the way.

4. Celebrate Successes: Acknowledge and celebrate their accomplishments, no matter how small. Recognize their cfforts and provide positive reinforcement. Celebrating successes boosts morale and encourages continued progress.

5. Constructive Feedback: Offer feedback that is constructive and supportive. Focus on areas of

improvement while highlighting their strengths. This approach helps individuals learn and grow without feeling overwhelmed or discouraged.

6. Promote Self-Care: Encourage individuals to prioritize self-care and well-being. Remind them of the importance of taking breaks, managing stress, and maintaining a healthy work-life balance. Self-care contributes to overall resilience and motivation.

By implementing these strategies, you can provide individuals with the support they need to overcome feelings of hopelessness and discouragement. Remember, everyone's journey is unique, so it's important to tailor your approach to their specific needs and circumstances.

The above-mentioned essentials are the best tools I've found to build a bridge that helps people struggling to see a clear path to the other side of what they're currently feeling and/or experiencing.

So, when given the opportunity to build this bridge, do the following: employ empathy, active listening, effective communication, validation, problem-solving, support, and patience.

Even though all these skills are essential, the focus of this book will be on the when, what, and how of **encouragement**. I recommend reading it in bite-sized chunks (maybe more like a devotional) for best results.

Reaching that level of leadership requires you to master the five essentials, and that takes time; it is not a quick fix. While we won't delve into the details of these steps here, they are as follows:

The goal of this book is to help you become a perpetual encourager and ultimately a master empowerer. Reaching that level of leadership is a continuous process and will involve you mastering the 5 essentials mentioned earlier. Again, it will take time, so be patient. Remain open to learning more about the five essentials over time and how they can contribute to your growth as a perpetual encourager and, ultimately, a master empowerer.

Below, I've outlined a thoughtful and comprehensive approach to leadership and personal development. The concept of being a "perpetual" in each step suggests a continuous and ongoing commitment to these principles. Here's a breakdown of each step and its significance:

Level #1: The Perpetual Engager
Building strong connections and relationships is crucial for effective leadership. Fostering open communication and creating an inclusive environment can lead to better teamwork, trust, and a sense of belonging among team members.

Level #2: The Perpetual Encourager
Providing ongoing support and motivation helps individuals overcome challenges and reach their potential. Positive reinforcement can boost morale and productivity, leading to a more positive and resilient team.

Level #3: The Perpetual Educator
Continuous learning and development are essential for personal and professional growth. Sharing knowledge,

insights, and skills with others creates a culture of learning and improvement within the team or organization.

Level #4: The Perpetual Equipper
Providing the necessary tools, resources, and opportunities empowers individuals to enhance their abilities and achieve their goals. This step emphasizes the importance of enabling others to succeed through access to the right resources.

Level #5: The Master Empowerer
Reaching the highest level of leadership by empowering others to become leaders themselves is the pinnacle of this approach. Delegating responsibilities, trusting others, and creating a culture of autonomy and shared success can lead to a more self-sufficient and high-performing team.

By following these steps, one can create a leadership style that is focused on building strong relationships, supporting others, fostering growth, and empowering the team to achieve their full potential.

Once again, the book focuses on defining the importance of encouragement in leadership, providing practical techniques and strategies for offering genuine encouragement, and emphasizing the creation of a culture that values and practices encouragement at all levels of the organization. We will cover real-life examples and address common challenges that will help you understand and implement Essential #2: Encouragement.

I acknowledge that many people have experienced moments when they had a Big Hairy Audacious Goal (BHAG) but didn't pursue it due to a lack of encouragement or even discouragement from others. By focusing on the importance of encouragement, this book aims to empower individuals to overcome such obstacles and pursue their goals with confidence and determination. It provides insights, strategies, and practical advice to both readers and leaders, highlighting the transformative power of encouragement in achieving personal and collective success.

Challenge:

Before we begin, I want to issue you a challenge. Accepting this challenge now will be key to understanding this book.

Ready: Raise both your hands as high as you possibly can. Ready...Up! Hold for 5 seconds—1001, 1002, 1003, 1004, 1005. Now, drop them! Remember this small exercise because we will come back to it at the end of the book.

Chapter 5: Prerequisites for a Perpetual Encourager

To become a perpetual encourager, there are several prerequisites that need to be acknowledged and embraced:

1) Willingness to engage people where they stand: This means being open to connecting with others at their current level and understanding their unique circumstances, perspectives, and needs. It involves meeting people where they are without imposing preconceived notions or judgments.

2) Willingness to listen to their story without judgment: Being a perpetual encourager requires active and empathetic listening. It means creating a safe and non-judgmental space for individuals to share their experiences, challenges, and aspirations. By genuinely hearing their story, you can better understand their journey and provide meaningful support.

3) Willingness to learn: Continuous learning is essential to becoming a perpetual encourager. It involves recognizing

that people's needs, circumstances, and aspirations can vary widely. By actively seeking knowledge, insights, and understanding, you can expand your perspective and develop the capacity to provide relevant and meaningful encouragement.

These prerequisites are crucial because they form the foundation of effective encouragement. Ignoring them can make it challenging to fulfill the role of a perpetual encourager. By embracing these prerequisites, you can cultivate an environment of support, empathy, and growth, both for yourself and others.

Perpetual encouragers at their core are always on the hunt for the opportunity to lift the spirit of others. However, they sometimes find it challenging to properly respond to these opportunities when they find them. Opportunities to encourage others are often found in people who are struggling for varied reasons. Responding to their needs can be easy at times, while other times, it will take courage, concern, and commitment for you to **engage** with and **encourage** the individual.

Even though this book is only focused on Essential #2, it is important that you under Essential #1: Engage.

4) The Most Important Prerequisite: Learning to Engage: Engaging with others and offering encouragement can indeed make a significant difference in their lives. Recognizing opportunities to engage and encourage individuals who have experienced loss, career stagnation, fear of change, abuse, or who are transitioning to new roles is crucial for effective leadership and support.

Developing essential skills such as active listening, empathy, patience, and compassion will enable you to connect with others on a deeper level, understand their challenges, and provide meaningful support and encouragement. By honing these skills, you can create a more supportive and empowering environment for those around you.

Remember that genuine engagement and encouragement can have a profound impact on individuals, helping them overcome obstacles, regain confidence, and achieve their potential.

Skills to Develop:

Develop your listening skills, your empathy, your patience, and your compassion, and you will be ready.

There are many skills that go into being a perpetual encourager. I'm going to cover 4 key skills that I think are absolutely essential in this regard.

1. Understands Leadership

It's essential for perpetual encouragers to have a deep understanding of the responsibilities and expectations of leadership. This understanding applies not only to titled or positional leaders but also to individuals who have the capacity to influence others through relationships and interactions. Leadership is measured by the level of influence one has in any given situation, and the teachings in this book are aimed at helping individuals maximize their influence, regardless of their specific leadership role.

The principles outlined in the book can be applied in various contexts, whether it's a boardroom, a classroom, or your chosen field of play (any other setting) where you have the opportunity to positively impact others. By committing this principle to memory and consistently applying it, you can enhance your influence and become a more effective leader, fostering a culture of encouragement and empowerment in your respective environments.

2. Commit and Invest in Yourself

The path to becoming a perpetual encourager starts with a commitment to invest in yourself before extending that investment to others. Gaining trust and respect from those you aim to lead, encourage, and empower is crucial for long-term success, and this process cannot be rushed. It's essential to lead yourself successfully before leading others, making the necessary investment in personal growth and development.

Becoming a perpetual encourager requires time and commitment, regardless of your level of talent and ability. There are no shortcuts or ways to bypass the process, as time is the great equalizer. "The Encouragement Factor: Give Me One More Inch" can serve as an excellent resource to begin this journey, providing valuable insights and guidance for those seeking to enhance their ability to encourage and empower others.

3. You Are the Thermostat

To bring out the best in your team and achieve optimal results, it's crucial to accept responsibility for every aspect of your team's culture and performance. As a leader, you must act as a thermostat, setting the temperature and tone for the team, rather than merely reflecting it like a thermometer. Your dedication, desire, and drive for success should be on par with or greater than that of your team. By being an exemplary leader and setting the tone, you can inspire and motivate your team to perform at their highest potential.

Your commitment and execution as a leader play a significant role in fostering the release of your team's fullest potential. By setting a clear example, providing inspiration, and fostering a culture of high achievement, you can empower your team to strive for excellence and reach the highest levels of performance.

4. Possess an Inspiring Vision

Having an inspiring vision for your team is essential. Attempting to encourage others with an uninspiring vision can lead to a negative impact, affecting each team member. It's crucial that your vision and leadership are inspiring, as this will ultimately motivate and inspire your team.

If you find yourself lacking motivation or passion for leading and encouraging your team, it's important to engage in self-reflection and self-assessment to understand the underlying reasons for these feelings. If you realize that you cannot fully commit to the work of leading and inspiring your team, it may be necessary to reevaluate your vision and your role as a leader. You may need to either step up and lead with renewed commitment or make room for someone else to take the lead, ensuring that the team is led by someone who can provide the necessary inspiration and direction.

1. 7 Questions to Ask Yourself

These seven questions provide a valuable framework for leaders to assess and evaluate their current vision, team, and leadership dynamics.

Here's a brief overview of each question:

1. Does my current vision have any intrinsic value (matter) to the team?

Assess whether your vision is meaningful and relevant to your team. An impactful vision should resonate with team members and inspire them to work towards a common goal.

2. Is my current team invested in bringing the vision to life?

Evaluate the level of commitment and enthusiasm your team demonstrates toward realizing the vision. Team buy-in and dedication are crucial for achieving shared goals.

3. Am I leading a team that needs a roster overhaul (wrong people/wrong position)?

Consider whether the composition of your team aligns with the vision and whether adjustments are necessary to ensure that the right people are in the right roles.

4. Does my team have the necessary skills to carry out the vision?

Assess whether your team possesses the requisite skills and capabilities to effectively execute the vision. Identify any skill gaps that need to be addressed.

5. Does my current organization and I share a common vision?

Examine whether your vision aligns with the overarching goals and direction of your organization. Alignment with the organizational vision is essential for coherence and synergy.

6. Do I have the necessary resources and support to fulfill the vision?

Determine whether you have access to the required resources, support, and infrastructure to enable the realization of your vision.

7. Should I be leading this team?

Reflect on whether you are the right leader for the team and the vision at hand. This question prompts introspection regarding your fit as the team's leader.

If one or more of these questions elicit a "yes," it's important to develop a comprehensive game plan to address each factor, eliminating or minimizing any persistent obstacles. By proactively addressing these factors, leaders can create an environment conducive to reaching their fullest potential and fostering their team's success.

2. *Ensure Intrinsic Value*

Aligning the team's vision with your own as a leader is crucial for achieving success. When team members don't fully buy into the vision, it can lead to disengagement, lack of motivation, and ultimately hinder the team's performance. Reframing the vision to align with the needs, wants, and goals of the team is an essential step in fostering a sense of ownership and commitment among team members.

Here are a few steps to consider when reframing your vision to align with your team's needs:

1. Understand the Team's Perspective: Take the time to listen to your team members and understand their perspectives, concerns, and aspirations. This will help you identify where the misalignment exists and gain valuable insights into what matters most to your team.

2. Communicate Openly: Transparent communication is key to gaining buy-in from your team. Clearly communicate your vision and, more importantly, be open to feedback. Engage in two-way communication to ensure that the vision is a result of collective input.

3. Identify Common Goals: Find common ground between your vision and the team's goals. Highlight how the vision can help team members achieve their individual and

collective objectives and demonstrate the value it brings to them.

4. Empower Team Members: Involve your team in the development of the vision and empower them to contribute to its refinement. When team members feel that their input is valued and integrated into the vision, they are more likely to embrace it.

5. Provide Context: Help your team understand the "why" behind the vision. When team members understand the rationale and purpose behind the vision, they are more likely to connect with it on a deeper level.

6. Celebrate Small Wins: As the team begins to align with the reframed vision, acknowledge and celebrate small victories. Recognizing progress reinforces the team's commitment and fosters a sense of accomplishment.

By taking these steps, you can work towards creating a shared vision that resonates with your team, leading to increased motivation, collaboration, and ultimately, higher levels of success for the entire team.

3. *Wrong Seat on the Bus?*

This is a death sentence to any team. If you are not the correct leader or you have a team made up of the wrong people, you must move quickly to correct this situation. I refer to this as the *Bus Ticket Syndrome*. You **must** first verify whether you are the right leader. If you are not, then remove yourself and seek to find your right place. Ensuring the right leadership and team composition is crucial for a team's success. Like "getting the right people on the bus," it's important to assess whether leaders and team members are in the right roles. This is a concept made popular by Jim Collins in *Good to Great*.

This may involve seeking feedback, making changes where necessary, and carefully considering the skills needed for each role. Effective leadership and a well-composed team are essential for achieving organizational goals. This may require you to get outside opinions/feedback. So, if you are the right leader, then move forward into the driver's seat.

Next, you need to evaluate whether you have the right people on the bus you're driving. If someone on the bus doesn't have a ticket (i.e., doesn't fit or doesn't possess the applicable or transferable skills), then they need to be removed (coached out or fired) from the bus. If someone on the bus has a ticket, but they're sitting in the wrong seat (i.e., possess skills valuable to the team, but are placed in the wrong role), then you must instruct them (coach up) to move into the correct seat. The next step is to find (recruit) the people who can fill the now vacated seats. *Don't rush this step!* Take the necessary time needed to clearly identify all the seats (roles and skills) on your bus (team). Then get the correct ticket (opportunity) to the correct ticket holder (team member).

Biggest Challenge:

Don't be afraid to revoke some tickets and make other new seat assignments.*

**Exercise: List required skills and compare it to your team's actual list of current skills. If some functions or tasks are required to accomplish your vision, but no one on your team can perform them, you must immediately begin hiring/selecting individuals who* *possess the missing skills/talents or train the existing team members to do those functions and tasks.*

4. *One Bus - Same Page*

Remember, there is only one bus, so once you get people into their seats, ensure that everyone is on the same page. No team will experience consistent success unless team members are on the same page. If team members do not share a common vision, their efforts will be diluted, and the team will ultimately come up short of its mission. To avoid this scenario, solicit feedback from your team regarding their buy-in, commitment, and alignment to the vision. To ensure that vision alignment is strong, consistently undertake formal and informal research and ascertain what is vital to the team members. Once you get this information, incorporate it when appropriate into the overall vision. This will increase the team's dedication, commitment, and overall achievement.

When possible, incorporate things that you know motivate and inspire your team into the overall vision. Once you understand their vision and construct a picture around it, you can effectively help them link their vision with the team's vision. Once you've successfully done this, you will have the makings of a unified, self-motivated, and engaged team, which, as we mentioned earlier, is crucial for overall success. Once they are fully engaged, and once you are fully engaged as their leader, then you'll be ready to be their biggest fan—or better yet, their perpetual encourager!

In summary, to ensure team success, communicate the vision clearly and seek feedback from team members to ensure alignment. Incorporate elements that motivate and inspire your team into the overall vision. Provide continual encouragement and support to keep the team engaged and motivated.

Although these guidelines will give you a head start, you still need to be aware that this is only the beginning. Achieving a vision will never be a straight-forward and effortless process; the passage of time causes motivation to falter, inspiration to fade, and dedication to fluctuate. You can minimize these side effects by keeping your team informed about the mission and the necessary steps required to achieve said mission. This can be done through clear, concise, and consistent communication that builds consensus and buy-in. One of the most important facets of this process is to solicit feedback and ensure a general comprehension of the overall vision. Don't ever assume that everyone fully understands the vision.*

**Application: The more clarity each team member has regarding the vision and their specific role in achieving it, the better the team's results will be. Maintain constant, clear, and innovative communication until everyone is on the same page. Then rinse and repeat as often as needed.*

5. *Strategic Team Diversity*

It makes no difference how much talent or ability your team possesses if they don't fully encompass the vision. The importance of a shared vision and diverse perspectives within a team or organization can't be minimized. Indeed, a clear and compelling vision can serve as a guiding force for a team, aligning its efforts and motivating its members. However, it's also crucial to recognize that a diversity of skills, abilities, and personalities is essential for a team's overall success.

Embracing diversity within a team can bring a wide range of perspectives and approaches to problem-solving, leading to more creative and effective solutions. Each team member's unique strengths and experiences can contribute to the team's overall capability and resilience. As a result, effective leadership involves not only casting a vision but also fostering an environment where diverse contributions are valued and integrated.

Young and inexperienced leaders sometimes struggle with this concept. Inexperienced leaders may initially seek out team members who share their perspectives and approaches, believing this will lead to cohesion and efficiency. However, this can limit the team's ability to adapt, innovate, and address complex challenges. Over time, leaders often come to appreciate the value of diverse perspectives and learn to build teams with complementary skills and experiences.

The sooner you recognize that a team is about *strategic diversity*, and that each member has a unique set of skills that they bring to their roles, you will begin seeing incredible results. A team is much like the human body—no matter how healthy your heart is, the human body can't function if a heart is all it has.

To fully function as human beings, we require all our organs to perform their unique purpose. Likewise, all successful leaders require each team member to uniquely contribute to the overall mission and must energize, engage, and empower them with the opportunities to do so.

Successful leaders fully understand the importance of ***strategic team diversity***. This concept creates an environment where each member's unique contributions are appreciated and celebrated. Underestimating the value of having a diverse collection of people with a diverse range of talents and skills on your team will impede your overall success. Building a diverse team and ensuring that each member is engaged, encouraged, educated, equipped, and empowered is crucial for overall success. This approach fosters a supportive and inclusive environment where each individual's talents and skills can be effectively utilized, leading to a more capable and high-performing team.

6. The Importance of Vision Alignment

Success is never guaranteed! You can still come up short of your team's goals and vision, even if your team is comprised of the best and most qualified people. Lou Holtz summed it up in this way, "To win, you must have outstanding athletes. Whoever the coach is, I couldn't care less. Without great athletes, you cannot win consistently, but you can still lose with them. This is when coaching shines." Indeed, without effective leadership, even a highly skilled, motivated, supported, trained, and empowered team can still be at risk of failing to achieve its goals. This underscores the crucial role of a leader and highlights the necessity for continuous personal and professional development to guide both yourself and your team towards success. Leaders must be committed to ongoing growth and improvement to effectively lead their teams to greatness.

Effective leadership is critical for turning a group of individuals into a successful team. Vision alignment is a key aspect of this. Great leaders are able to articulate a compelling vision that inspires and motivates their team members. They understand the importance of aligning individual and collective goals with the overall vision of the organization.

In addition to vision alignment, effective leaders also possess effective communication skills, empathy, and the ability to empower their team members. They create an environment where individuals feel valued, challenged, and supported, which ultimately contributes to the success of the team as a whole.

Furthermore, great coaching plays a significant role in developing the skills and capabilities of team members. Through coaching, leaders can provide guidance, feedback, and opportunities for growth, which not only benefits the individuals but also contributes to the overall performance and success of the team.

Overall, effective leadership is about creating a shared sense of purpose, fostering collaboration, and empowering individuals to contribute their best to the team's success. It is a multifaceted role that requires a combination of a strategic vision, interpersonal skills, and an understanding of how to bring out the best in others.

Certainly, having talent, buy-in, unity, and strategic team diversity are critical components for a team's success. However, vision alignment and strong leadership are equally essential for sustainable success.

Vision alignment ensures that all team members are working towards a common goal, and it provides a sense of direction and purpose. A strong leader plays a pivotal role in fostering this alignment by clearly communicating the vision, building consensus, and inspiring others to commit to the shared objectives.

In addition to communication, a strong leader engages with team members to understand their perspectives, encourages them to contribute their ideas and insights, educates them about the vision and strategy, equips them with the necessary resources and support, and empowers them to take ownership of their roles and responsibilities.

By providing this guidance and support, a strong leader can help the team navigate challenges, adapt to changes, and effectively execute plans. Ultimately, it's the leader's ability to cultivate a shared vision and empower the team that can significantly impact the team's ability to engage and succeed.

Engagement is Mission Critical

Engagement, as the starting point, is indeed crucial for building a successful and cohesive team. When team members are engaged, they are more likely to be committed and motivated, leading to improved productivity and a positive work environment.

Moving from engagement to empowerment involves a process of enabling and supporting team members to take on more responsibility and make meaningful contributions. This transition requires leaders to provide encouragement, offer opportunities for education and skill development, and ensure that team members are equipped with the resources and support they need to succeed.

Understanding the importance of engagement and mastering the essentials of encouragement, education, equipping, and empowerment can indeed lay a solid foundation for effective leadership. By prioritizing these elements, leaders can create a culture of trust, collaboration, and growth within their teams, ultimately leading to greater success for both the team and the organization as a whole.

Review of the 4 Essentials

These elements are crucial for understanding how to lead and empower a team effectively. I can't emphasize it enough; you must have a full understanding of the dynamic nature of applying these essentials and tailoring them to your team's makeup and maturity level. It highlights the need for flexibility in your leadership approach. Let's delve into a brief review of the four essentials before moving into the main focus of encouragement.

1. Engagement: This involves getting the team members actively involved, committed, and emotionally invested in the work at hand. Engaged team members are more likely to be motivated and productive, leading to better overall performance.

2. Education: Providing the necessary knowledge, skills, and resources to the team members to enable them to perform their tasks effectively. Continuous learning and development are crucial for both individual and team growth.

3. Equipment: Ensuring that the team has the necessary tools, technology, and resources to carry out their responsibilities efficiently. Well-equipped teams are better positioned to succeed and innovate.

4. Empowerment: Granting the team members the authority, autonomy, and trust to make decisions and take ownership of their work. Empowered teams are often more creative, adaptive, and motivated, leading to higher levels of performance and satisfaction.

It's clear that these essentials are interrelated and form the foundation for effective leadership and team performance. Your approach to tailoring their application based on the team's needs and the specific goal at hand demonstrates a full understanding of leadership dynamics.

Having a working understanding of these essentials and being able to integrate them into your leadership process is crucial for effectively leading teams. Continuous learning and daily practice are key components in developing the necessary skills to apply these essentials in a leadership role. If you walk away with nothing else, continually educate yourself on these principles and consistently put them into practice as part of your leadership toolbox.

This book was written for leaders or individuals who want to learn the power of the Encouragement Factor! We will continue that journey by diving deeper into the Encouragement Factor, exploring how it can help you become a perpetual encourager!

There is no one amongst the living who doesn't require encouragement at some point on their journey. Encouragement is a powerful tool in leadership and personal development. It's true that even the most driven and successful individuals can benefit from encouragement and support. In fact, sometimes those who appear the most self-assured or accomplished are the ones who need it the most. Even the most callous, hard-headed, self-made individuals can sometimes require encouragement to remain on track and progress toward their goals. Everyone faces challenges, self-doubt, and moments of difficulty, regardless of their outward appearance or level of success.

Even though this is not news to most, it (encouragement as a leadership tool) unfortunately falls through the cracks or fails to be implemented on a daily basis. We tend to think that certain groups of people don't need to be motivated and encouraged. But this is very wrong; we all need encouragement!

By acknowledging the value of encouragement and actively implementing it in our daily interactions, we can create a more inclusive and uplifting environment, both in the workplace and in our personal lives.

Encouragement is a universal need that transcends individual accomplishments or perceived self-sufficiency. In both personal and professional contexts, the provision of encouragement is a fundamental aspect of effective leadership. By understanding the importance of encouragement and actively incorporating it into daily interactions, leaders can cultivate the type of environment that fosters buy-in and ownership.

Recognizing and fully understanding that even the most successful and self-reliant individuals benefit from encouragement, leaders can play a pivotal role in fostering a supportive and collaborative community. Embracing encouragement as a leadership tool not only motivates individuals to excel but also contributes to a more positive and fulfilling work or social environment. When leaders actively promote a culture of encouragement, they inspire those around them to strive for their best, ultimately leading to increased productivity, engagement, and overall well-being.

As leaders, we must change our attitude or relationship with encouragement. We need to become encouraging leaders. This will improve our overall performance as leaders, while also enhancing our satisfaction in every area of our lives—from leader to team member to parent to family.

To get to where we want to go in life, we all benefit from encouraging words from those around us, like our friends, family, teachers, and mentors. Most successful people have benefitted from a strong support system that has assisted them in achieving success in life, whether it was formal or informal.

It makes no difference who we highlight: Tiger Woods, Serena Williams, Michael Jordan, or even Jesus. Each of these individuals had encouragers at key points throughout their life. Michael Jordan, Tiger Woods, and Serena Williams all had fathers who significantly contributed to their success in the sports world. Jesus had loving parents and an older cousin, John the Baptist, who encouraged Him.

Hopefully, you've received some wonderful words of support from family or friends during a challenging time. Whether it's a student aiming for an A+ on that final exam or a brand-new entrepreneur launching the next Tesla, the encouragement of friends and family can and will help you succeed.

Unfortunately, there are moments in life when we all overlook this easy to execute responsibility of encouraging others.

Offering words of encouragement can positively impact those around us by boosting their confidence, motivation, and resilience. Taking the time to express belief in someone's abilities or efforts can make a meaningful difference in their lives.

By providing support and expressing belief in someone's abilities or efforts, we can help bolster their confidence, motivation, and resilience. This can be especially crucial during challenging times or when individuals are working towards personal or professional goals. The ripple effect of encouragement can lead to improved morale, stronger relationships, and a more supportive and empathetic community overall. Therefore, it's important to recognize the significance of offering genuine and heartfelt words of encouragement, as they can often resonate deeply and have a lasting effect on the recipients.

Reflect on Your Daily Interactions

These are insightful questions and potential responses that can help you reflect on your interactions with others and your own behavior regarding encouragement.

1. When was the last time I offered words of encouragement (unsolicited or unprovoked by a special occasion)?

Reflect on recent interactions with friends, family, colleagues, or even strangers. Think about instances where you provided support, praise, or motivation without being prompted. Consider both verbal and written forms of communication.

2. How often do I go above and beyond to encourage others?

Consider your general approach to supporting others. Think about specific instances where you've made an extra effort to uplift or motivate someone. This could include offering assistance, providing emotional support, or simply being present for others in meaningful ways.

3. Do I freely and consistently offer encouraging words and advice?

Reflect on your communication style and whether you tend to offer positive and supportive words regularly. Consider whether you actively seek out opportunities to provide encouragement or if it tends to be more reactive based on specific situations.

By contemplating these questions, you can gain a deeper understanding of your own behavior and identify areas for personal growth when it comes to offering encouragement and support to others.

If you had to spend a significant amount of time thinking of an answer to these questions, then continue reading. Leaders who understand the fundamental importance of encouragement possess a powerful tool for fostering positive environments and achieving outstanding results. In any setting, whether it's a workplace, community organization, or educational institution, the ability to effectively encourage and empower others is a hallmark of successful leadership.

Moreover, leaders who naturally embody this trait have the opportunity to create lasting impacts on the lives of those they lead. Encouragement serves as a catalyst for growth, motivation, and resilience.

It's crucial for leaders to continually absorb information and advice about the significance of encouragement, as it can serve as a reminder of the profound impact their words and actions can have on others. By understanding and embracing the foundational nature of encouragement in leadership, individuals in positions of influence can cultivate a culture of support, growth, and empowerment within their spheres of influence. Many leaders forget or don't know just how essential encouragement is—or better yet, foundational—it is to be an empowering leader, especially if encouragement comes naturally to them.

I've spent countless hours mentoring leaders on how to maximize their skills and how to utilize numerous tools and resources. While these leaders have varied in their experience, scope, and overall ability, I always walk away from these encounters with a renewed respect and appreciation for the power of encouragement.

"Wise (encouraging) speech is rarer and more valuable than gold and rubies." - Proverbs 20:15

6 Lessons of Encouragement

1. *Encouragement releases potential.*

When we encourage others, we communicate what we believe about them, and we reinforce the notion that we believe they have what it takes to succeed. This encouragement does not imply that everything is perfect or easy, but that the potential for them to develop and improve is possible.

It establishes a foundation upon which to build. When we encourage others, they become more conscious of other's positive perception of them, which, in turn, helps them better comprehend their circumstances and the potential opportunities that exist before them.

2. *Encouragement builds a foundation of belief.*

When we realize that others believe in us, everything changes. This is why it is important that leaders are encouragers. Just a few positive words of belief can be the difference between success or failure. We so often seek to correct the failures of others, when alternatively, we could have simply encouraged them, which holds the potential to prevent the failure.

When we encourage others, we communicate that we value what they have accomplished and, by extension, believe in what they can accomplish in the future. This strengthens their belief in themselves and empowers them to reach their full potential.

3. *Encouragement fosters confidence and self-esteem.* Give encouragement frequently, because receiving compliments on a job well done and hearing how their work makes a difference can indeed boost the confidence of those you lead. Recognition and positive feedback from others can validate one's efforts, reinforce their sense of achievement, and provide motivation to continue making valuable contributions. When individuals receive acknowledgment for their work, it significantly impacts their confidence, sense of purpose, and overall satisfaction with their efforts.

As leaders, we are confidence builders, and this confidence will be rewarded in a more engaged and confident team member. A more confident and engaged team member will generally result in increased productivity, innovation, and execution. Confidence and self-esteem rise when we are encouraged. The encouragement may provide a brief boost, or permanently change someone's confidence. In either case, the encouragement matters. You never know when what you say will significantly impact someone's confidence and self-esteem, so let those words of encouragement flow!

"Kind words are like honey-sweet to the soul and healthy for the body." –Prov 16:24

4. Encouragement helps improve attitude.

No one wants to feel unsupported and isolated. Often, these feelings lead to a less than desirable attitude and mindset, which then spreads like cancer, beginning with one person and spreading throughout the entire team. But a quick antidote for this is simply sharing a few encouraging words.

When appropriately applied, encouragement makes us feel better. It's hard for your team members to feel anxious, angry, or sad when there is a spring in their step, a smile on their face, and laughter in their heart. You hold the key to releasing these emotions, ultimately eradicating any forms of long-term sadness or anger. Not only will your team perform better when you encourage them, but they will also be healthier, happier, and more productive when they adopt a positive mindset, and work in an environment that fuels optimism.

"A cheerful disposition is good for your health; gloom & doom leave you bone-tired." - Pro 17:22

5. *Encouragement motivates people to take action.* Sometimes, it can be difficult to move forward, take action, or try something new.

Encouragement is a powerful force that can greatly influence an individual's willingness to take action and embrace new opportunities. In our journey through life, there are often moments when we encounter challenges or face the prospect of trying something new, and it is during these times that the impact of encouragement becomes especially significant.

When individuals receive positive encouragement from those around them, it can have a profound effect on their mindset and outlook. Genuine words of support, affirmation, and belief in their abilities can serve to bolster their confidence, enhance their belief in themselves, and elevate their overall attitude. This, in turn, can unlock their potential and empower them to take the necessary steps toward their goals.

Conversely, a lack of encouragement or the presence of persistent negativity can have detrimental effects on an individual's mindset. When individuals do not receive the support and encouragement they need, it can lead to self-doubt, diminished confidence, and a reluctance to take action. Over time, this can erode their sense of potential and willingness to pursue new endeavors.

It's important to recognize that the impact of encouragement goes beyond mere words. Genuine encouragement is a catalyst for empowerment, and it can inspire individuals to step out of their comfort zones, embrace challenges, and strive for growth. When people feel supported and uplifted, they are more likely to believe in their abilities and approach new opportunities with a positive and determined mindset.

Therefore, as members of a community, whether it be in our families, workplaces, or social circles, it is crucial to cultivate an environment where positive encouragement is abundant. By doing so, we can help individuals realize their potential, nurture their belief in themselves, bolster their confidence, and foster an attitude of determination and resilience.

In essence, the more encouragement individuals receive, the more empowered and willing they are to act.

"Words kill, words give life; they're either poison or fruit—you choose." – Prov. 18:21

6. *One size doesn't fit all.*

Everyone is not at the same level of inner security or self-esteem, and so, some may require more encouragement than others.

Don't allow those in a difficult place to contaminate your perspective nor diminish your willingness to encourage as needed. The people you work with and lead are individuals, and you must see them as such. Don't ever forget that everyone benefits from real, genuine, and intentional support, and it is your responsibility to provide this.

Now, imagine for a moment that your one act of encouragement fosters the development of a positive, confident, self-assured person, striving to reach their maximum potential. How powerful would that be? That is what genuine, true, and meaningful encouragement does.

These six lessons apply to anyone in any situation. If your desire as a coaching leader is to help others become their best, you must become a perpetual encourager. Once you begin using encouragement consistently and successfully in your role as a coaching leader, you will come to realize that encouragement is one of the most potent tools in your leadership toolbox. Don't underestimate the power of your words—they hold the power of life (encouragement) and death (defeat). Choose to speak life and encouragement. Now, let's dig a little deeper and see what Merriam-Webster has to say about encouragement:

<u>ENCOURAGEMENT:</u>

Encouragement is the act of inspiring and uplifting others through words, actions, or gestures. It involves providing support, motivation, and optimism to help someone feel empowered and confident in their abilities.

Encouragement can be expressed through kind words, listening attentively, offering praise and recognition, and offering assistance or guidance when needed. It helps to boost someone's self-esteem, improve their outlook, and foster a positive mindset, which can lead to increased productivity, resilience, and overall well-being.

Application: When coaching or leading, remember the value and effectiveness of encouragement, regardless of the individual's ability, experience, or previous accomplishments.

Chapter 11: Incorporate Encouragement into Your Daily Leadership

All successful leaders have the ability to incorporate encouragement into their leadership strategy. The next few pages will discuss how you can incorporate encouragement into your day-to-day leadership. Ironically, being a perpetual encourager isn't just about encouraging others, but it is also about your ability to receive encouragement.

When you constantly encourage others, it creates a positive and uplifting environment. However, it is equally important to be open to receiving encouragement yourself. By allowing others to support and uplift you, you not only validate their efforts but also acknowledge your own worth and capabilities.

Receiving encouragement can be challenging for some individuals. It may stem from a fear of vulnerability or a belief that they don't deserve recognition. However, embracing encouragement is crucial for personal growth and self-belief.

When you accept encouragement, you demonstrate humility and gratitude. It shows that you value and appreciate the efforts of others. By accepting their positive words or gestures, you reinforce the idea that you are deserving of encouragement, just like anyone else.

Moreover, your ability to receive encouragement can be a powerful source of motivation. When others believe in you and express their support, it boosts your confidence and self-esteem. It reminds you of your own capabilities and encourages you to push beyond your limits.

Believing in your own abilities is another essential aspect of being a perpetual encourager. It is about recognizing your strengths, embracing your weaknesses, and having faith in your potential. When you trust in yourself, you radiate confidence, which inspires and encourages others.

By believing in your abilities, you set an example for those around you. Your self-assurance becomes contagious, motivating others to have confidence in themselves as well. This creates a cycle of encouragement and empowerment, where everyone uplifts and supports one another.

In conclusion, being a perpetual encourager goes beyond just uplifting others. It involves being open to receiving encouragement, acknowledging your worth, and believing in your own abilities. By embracing encouragement and having faith in yourself, you create a positive environment that fosters personal growth and empowers those around you.

There are 3 primary approaches to incorporating encouragement into your life as a leader:

- Encouraging others
- Acknowledging the encouragement of others
- Believing in your own abilities

1. *Encouraging others*

Encouraging and inspiring others is a powerful and transformative act that can have a profound impact on individuals and communities. When we take the time to uplift and support those around us, we not only brighten their day but also contribute to creating a more positive world.

Here are some tips to help you become better at encouraging others:

1. Be genuine: When offering encouragement, be sincere and authentic. People can usually tell when someone is being insincere, so make sure your words and actions come from a genuine place.

2. Show empathy: Try to understand the other person's perspective and emotions. Empathizing with their struggles or challenges can help you provide more meaningful encouragement.

3. Be specific: Instead of giving generic compliments, be specific about what you appreciate or admire about the person or their actions. This shows that you have paid attention to their efforts and achievements.

4. Use positive language: Frame your encouragement in positive language. Instead of focusing on what someone

did wrong or could have done better, highlight their strengths and accomplishments.

5. Provide constructive feedback: Encouragement doesn't always mean just offering praise. Sometimes, it involves giving constructive feedback to help someone improve. However, make sure to balance criticism with positive reinforcement to maintain a supportive tone.

6. Be a good listener: Sometimes, people just need someone to listen to them without judgment or interruption. Practice active listening by giving your full attention, maintaining eye contact, and asking clarifying questions. This can be encouraging in itself.

7. Offer support: Encouragement can also come in the form of offering help or support. Let others know that you are there for them and are willing to assist them in any way you can.

8. Celebrate achievements: Acknowledge and celebrate the accomplishments of others. Whether big or small,

recognizing and celebrating milestones can provide a boost of encouragement and motivation.

9. Be patient: Everyone has their own pace and journey. Encouragement often requires patience, especially when someone is facing challenges or setbacks. Be patient with their progress and continue to offer support and encouragement.

10. Lead by example: Finally, be an encouraging role model. Show others how to uplift and support each other through your own words and actions. Your positive attitude and encouragement can inspire others to do the same.

Remember, encouragement is a powerful tool that can uplift and motivate others. By practicing these tips, you can become a source of support and positivity for those around you.

Remember every person you encounter may be fighting their own battles and facing their own set of unique challenges. In such a complex and often overwhelming world, your simple word of encouragement can provide the strength and motivation someone needs to keep going or to pursue their dreams.

Furthermore, the effects of encouragement often extend far beyond the immediate moment. Encouragement has the power to shift someone's mindset and enhance their overall well-being. When someone receives encouragement, they may begin to view themselves and their capabilities in a more positive light. This shift in perspective can lead to increased self-belief and confidence, which can be instrumental in achieving personal and professional goals.

Moreover, encouragement can open individuals' eyes to new opportunities and possibilities that they may not have previously considered. By hearing positive feedback and support from others, individuals may start to see their potential in areas they had not explored before. This can inspire them to step out of their comfort zone, take risks, and pursue their passions.

Additionally, encouragement can be a source of motivation and strength during challenging times. When faced with obstacles or setbacks, receiving support and encouragement can provide individuals with the determination and resilience needed to overcome these hurdles. It can remind them that they are not alone and that they have the ability to persevere.

In this culture of support and empowerment, people are more likely to take risks and pursue their goals because they know they have a community of people cheering them on. Encouragement becomes a driving force for personal growth and development.

Moreover, encouragement can also help individuals overcome self-doubt and build their confidence. When someone receives positive reinforcement and belief in their abilities, they start to believe in themselves as well. This newfound confidence can be transformative, enabling individuals to take on challenges they may have previously thought impossible.

Additionally, encouragement can be a powerful tool in building strong relationships and fostering a sense of belonging. When someone feels supported and encouraged by others, they are more likely to develop deeper connections and trust with those around them. Encouragement creates a positive and nurturing environment where people feel safe to be vulnerable and share their dreams and aspirations.

Furthermore, the act of encouraging others can be incredibly fulfilling and gratifying. Seeing someone flourish and succeed because of your support can bring immense joy and satisfaction. It strengthens the bond between individuals and fosters a sense of purpose in one's own life.

Overall, the ripple effect of encouragement is powerful and far-reaching. It has the potential to transform individuals, relationships, and entire communities. By cultivating a culture of support and empowerment, we can inspire others to believe in themselves, chase their dreams, and make positive changes in the world. In conclusion, encouragement is a powerful force that can have long-lasting effects on individuals. It can alter their perspective, boost their self-belief, and open doors to new opportunities.

Every opportunity to uplift and inspire others is an opportunity to make a meaningful difference in the world. By choosing to spread positivity and support, we create a ripple effect of kindness and empowerment that has the potential to transform lives and make the world a better place.

In conclusion, the impact of words of encouragement should never be underestimated. They have the power to boost self-confidence, foster a supportive environment, inspire resilience, and create positive change. By recognizing the value of our words and intentionally offering encouragement to others, we can make a significant difference in their lives and contribute to a more compassionate and uplifting world.

Your words of support and encouragement can have a profound impact on someone's journey towards achieving their goals. By acknowledging and highlighting someone's exceptional talent, you not only boost their confidence but also validate their abilities. This recognition can motivate them to continue honing their skills and pursuing their aspirations.

Similarly, if you come across someone who possesses enormous potential but is facing challenges or setbacks, your positive and encouraging words can make a significant difference. Sometimes, all it takes is a kind and uplifting message to remind them of their capabilities and instill the belief that they can overcome obstacles. Your support might be the catalyst they need to push through their struggles and keep striving towards their goals.

In both cases, your actions can unlock doors for individuals by providing them with the inspiration, motivation, and confidence to pursue their dreams. Your simple acts of support and encouragement can make a lasting impact and contribute to their personal and professional growth.

Sometimes, as leaders, we fear that sharing encouragement with others who have exceptional talent, enormous potential, or are on a similar path as ours could jeopardize our own opportunities or progress. When we genuinely encourage others, it creates a positive and supportive environment that benefits everyone involved. It fosters a sense of camaraderie and collaboration, allowing individuals to grow and excel together. By sharing our encouragement with others, we are not diminishing our own opportunities or progress but rather contributing to a collective success.

Moreover, encouraging others highlights our leadership abilities and demonstrates our confidence in our own skills. It shows that we are secure enough in our own abilities that we can uplift and support others without feeling threatened. This kind of mindset attracts respect and admiration from others, further enhancing our own reputation as leaders.

Encouragement should never be motivated by selfish intentions or the expectation of receiving something in return. Instead, it should come from a genuine desire to help others reach their full potential. When our encouragement is rooted in intrinsic value for the person, it becomes more authentic and impactful.

In summary, as leaders, it is essential to overcome any fear or hesitation we may have about sharing our encouragement with others. By doing so, we contribute to a positive and supportive environment, enhance our own leadership abilities, and create a ripple effect of positivity. So, let us encourage others because it is the right thing to do, and let the intrinsic value of our encouragement be the driving force behind our actions.

"Therefore encourage one another and build each other up, just as in fact you are doing." - 1 Thess. 5:11

2. *Acknowledgement of others' encouragement*

Have you ever met someone who can't seem to accept encouragement? There can be various reasons behind this behavior. Some individuals may have low self-esteem and struggle to believe the positive feedback they receive. They may have a negative self-image and find it difficult to accept praise or recognition.

Others may fear being seen as arrogant or boastful if they acknowledge their accomplishments. They may worry about how they will be perceived by others and prefer to downplay their achievements to avoid coming across as conceited.

Cultural and societal factors can also play a role. In certain cultures, accepting compliments (encouragement) graciously may be seen as immodest or self-centered. These individuals may have been raised with the belief that it is more humble or polite to deflect compliments (encouragement) rather than embrace them.

It is important to be understanding and patient with individuals who struggle to accept compliments. Consistently offering encouragement and reassurance can help them gradually become more comfortable with acknowledging their strengths and accomplishments.

Receiving encouragement from others helps build resilience. When faced with challenges or setbacks, hearing positive feedback from others can provide the motivation and determination needed to overcome obstacles. It reminds us that we have the support and belief of those around us, which can be incredibly empowering.

Additionally, accepting encouragement allows us to see ourselves through the eyes of others. Often, we are our own harshest critics and may not fully recognize our own achievements and capabilities. When others express their belief in us, it can help to shift our perspective and build self-confidence. This, in turn, allows us to take on new challenges and pursue opportunities that we may have otherwise doubted ourselves in.

In a professional context, receiving encouragement from colleagues and superiors can also lead to increased job satisfaction and engagement. Feeling valued and appreciated for our efforts can boost morale and create a positive work environment. It can also contribute to greater productivity and a willingness to go above and beyond in our work.

However, it's important to note that while receiving encouragement is beneficial, it's equally important to be able to internalize and believe in the positive feedback we receive. It's not enough to simply rely on external validation. We must also cultivate our own self-belief and confidence.

Receiving encouragement from others is crucial for personal and professional growth. It boosts confidence, fosters a supportive environment, builds resilience, and enhances job satisfaction. As leaders, it is important to accept and acknowledge the support of others, as it creates unity within the team and motivates team members to excel. So, embrace the encouragement and support from others, and use it as fuel to reach new heights.

When you receive encouragement on a team or joint project, it is important to acknowledge and appreciate it graciously. Instead of taking all the credit for yourself, redirect the credit to your team. Recognize their contributions and highlight their achievements. This not only shows humility but also fosters a culture of teamwork and collaboration.

By redirecting credit to the team, you demonstrate that you value their efforts and recognize that success is a collective effort. This can inspire your team members to continue putting in their best and feel a sense of ownership and pride in their work.

Moreover, redirecting credit to the team helps build trust and rapport among team members. It shows that you are not solely focused on personal recognition but are genuinely invested in the success and growth of the entire team. This can lead to increased motivation, loyalty, and dedication from your team members.

Additionally, when you redirect credit to the team, you create a culture of encouragement and support. If your team sees that you are willing to share credit and acknowledge their contributions, they are more likely to do the same for each other. This creates a positive and uplifting environment where team members feel appreciated and valued.

Let me explain!

For example, it is common for stage performers to deflect compliments when things do not go as planned during their performance. This behavior can be attributed to various reasons:

1. Perfectionism: Stage performers often strive for perfection in their craft, and when things do not meet their own lofty standards, they may feel dissatisfied with their performance. In such cases, they might deflect compliments to downplay any mistakes or imperfections.

2. Self-Criticism: Performers tend to be highly self-critical and may focus more on what went wrong rather than the overall success of their performance. They might feel that their flaws overshadow any positive aspects and, therefore, deflect compliments to avoid dwelling on those mistakes.

3. Professionalism: Some performers believe that accepting compliments despite a flawed performance may

come across as unprofessional. They may think it is more appropriate to acknowledge and discuss the areas that did not go as planned rather than accepting praise for an incomplete or imperfect show.

4. Humility: Many performers possess a humble nature and find it uncomfortable to accept compliments for a performance that did not meet their own expectations. They may feel that it is more genuine and honest to acknowledge their shortcomings rather than bask in undeserved praise.

It's important to note that the audience generally doesn't notice the insignificant things that a performer failed to do, or the trivial things that a performer accidentally did. One way to address this issue is by encouraging open communication within the team. This means creating a safe space where team members feel comfortable expressing their thoughts and ideas without fear of judgment or criticism. By fostering an environment of open communication, team members can feel more confident in sharing their accomplishments and accepting compliments from others.

Providing constructive feedback is another important aspect of addressing this issue. Instead of focusing solely on the imperfections, it is important to highlight the strengths and achievements of team members. By providing specific and constructive feedback, individuals can gain a better understanding of their abilities and accomplishments, which can help counteract their perfectionist tendencies.

Promoting a culture of acceptance and support is also crucial in addressing this issue. This involves creating an atmosphere where team members feel valued and appreciated for their contributions, regardless of any perceived imperfections. By promoting a culture of acceptance and support, team members are more likely to feel confident in their abilities and less likely to disparage themselves.

Finally, helping individuals recognize and manage their perfectionist tendencies can be beneficial. This can be done through workshops, coaching, or individual discussions. By helping individuals understand the negative impact of their perfectionism on themselves and the team, they can learn strategies to manage their tendencies more effectively. This may include setting realistic expectations, focusing on progress rather than solely on outcomes, and practicing self-compassion.

Overall, by fostering an environment of understanding and support, teams can work together to overcome the challenges posed by perfectionism. Through open communication, constructive feedback, and a culture of acceptance, teams can create a more positive and productive dynamic that allows individuals to thrive and contribute their best work.

Here is the other side of the coin when a perfectionist doesn't accept the compliment. When they react in this manner, they effectively communicate that the individual's opinion doesn't matter to them. This might be hurtful and discouraging for the individual offering encouragement from a well-intentioned place. When encouragement is consistently rejected, individuals may become discouraged and eventually stop offering support altogether. This can significantly impact the team's morale, productivity, and overall culture.

To prevent this from happening, it's crucial for team members to openly communicate about their needs and preferences regarding encouragement and feedback. Building a culture of open communication, mutual support, and constructive feedback can help prevent the discouragement and disengagement that can arise from a cycle of rejected encouragement.

As a leader within the organization, you play a key role in fostering a positive and supportive environment. You can encourage open dialogue, provide guidance on effective communication, and lead by example in both giving and receiving encouragement. By addressing these issues proactively, teams can maintain a culture of encouragement and support, which can ultimately contribute to their success and well-being.

Being open to receiving encouragement from others is an important aspect of fostering positive relationships and creating a supportive team environment. While humility and modesty are admirable qualities, it's essential to strike a balance and recognize the value of accepting positive affirmations and support from others.

When individuals accept encouragement as a gift, it not only benefits their own morale and well-being but also shows appreciation for the support offered by others. This creates a positive feedback loop that can contribute to a culture of mutual support and empowerment within a team or community.

Moreover, by being open to receiving encouragement, individuals can contribute to a positive work culture, which can lead to increased productivity and higher morale among team members. It also helps to promote a sense of camaraderie and mutual respect within the team, leading to a more cohesive and effective working environment.

Ultimately, the ability to receive encouragement can help individuals and teams thrive, creating a win-win scenario where both the recipient and the giver benefit from the positive exchange of support and affirmation!

"Two are better than one because they have a good reward for their toil. For if they fall, one will lift up his fellow. But woe to him who is alone when he falls and has not another to lift him up! Again, if two lie together, they keep warm, but how can one keep warm alone? And though a man might prevail against one who is alone, two will withstand him—a threefold cord is not quickly broken." - Ecc 4:9-12

3. *Believing in your abilities*

Now, you may be wondering, isn't believing in yourself synonymous with accepting encouragement? Not at all. It's true that there is a relationship between these two concepts, but they have a few differences.

Believing in yourself often involves having confidence in your own abilities, worth, and potential. This belief can be influenced by both internal and external factors. External encouragement from others can play a significant role in helping individuals develop and maintain belief in themselves. When others express belief in us, it can provide validation and support, which can, in turn, strengthen our own internal belief. Positive reinforcement and encouragement from others can help individuals overcome self-doubt and gain the confidence they need to pursue their goals.

However, it's also important for individuals to cultivate an internal sense of belief and self-confidence. This internal belief can come from various sources, including personal achievements, self-reflection, and a positive self-image. While external encouragement can be valuable, ultimately, individuals must develop their own sense of self-worth and confidence.

In summary, believing in oneself can be influenced by both internal and external factors, and accepting encouragement from others can play a vital role in nurturing and reinforcing this belief.

Encouragement, on the other hand, is an external belief others offer you. For those of us who lack the confidence to walk in a self-sustaining belief (intentionally or not), we rely on the encouragement of others. Once you've genuinely embraced it, absorbed it, and claimed it as truth, you'll be well on your way to believing in yourself. That's not always easy to do when you're facing rejection, hitting barrier, and things that aren't quite coming together the way you'd hoped—at least not yet!

Being a perpetual encourager requires effort and dedication. As a coach or leader, you must actively engage in the act of encouraging others. This involves providing positive reinforcement, celebrating achievements, and offering support and guidance when needed.

However, it is equally important to be able to receive encouragement yourself. This means being open to accepting compliments, acknowledging your own achievements, and allowing others to uplift and motivate you. By doing so, you not only boost your own confidence but also create an environment where encouragement flows freely.

Believing in yourself is crucial to becoming a perpetual encourager. Confidence in your abilities and strengths allows you to inspire and motivate others with authenticity and conviction. When you genuinely believe in yourself, your words and actions carry more weight and have a greater impact on those around you.

Once you have experienced the power and value of encouragement firsthand, you will naturally develop a desire to give and receive it from others. Encouragement becomes a cycle, where you inspire and uplift others, and in turn, they do the same for you. This creates a positive and supportive environment that fosters growth, development, and success.

In conclusion, to be a perpetual encourager as a coach or leader, you must actively engage in the work of encouraging, be open to receiving encouragement, and have confidence in yourself. By doing so, you create a culture of support and motivation that benefits both you and those you lead or coach.

Application: *Imagine you've been successful in your life, and you are fully aware of why you are doing what you are doing. You know that God has endowed you with a gift, a calling, or a message. You even have faith in it and believe it will happen, but then things don't unfold the way you anticipated them to. You are devastated and have no desire to move forward; your will to press on has suffered a major blow. What do you do in a moment like this?*

It's true that unexpected moments can bring about incredible opportunities for both leaders and team members. Sometimes, all it takes is for someone to stumble upon your story or gain deeper insight into your journey and goals. This newfound connection can lead to unexpected support and assistance from someone who genuinely wants to help you and contribute to your mission.

When someone expresses a desire to assist and becomes a sounding board for your thoughts, objectives, and aspirations, they become an invaluable encourager in your life. This person provides a different perspective, offers guidance, and serves as a source of motivation and inspiration. Their support can help you navigate challenges, overcome obstacles, and stay focused on your path to success.

This unexpected encouragement can have a profound impact on both your personal and professional growth. It boosts your confidence, strengthens your belief in yourself, and fuels your determination to achieve your goals. Additionally, having an encourager in your life can foster a sense of belonging and camaraderie, creating a supportive network that propels you forward.

It's important to embrace these unexpected moments and be open to receiving encouragement from others. Sometimes, the people who come into our lives unexpectedly can have the most significant impact. By accepting their support, you not only benefit from their guidance but also contribute to the positive energy and encouragement cycle that perpetuates growth and success.

In summary, unexpected moments can lead to incredible opportunities for leaders and team members. When someone discovers your story and expresses a desire to support your mission, they become an encourager in your life. Embrace these moments, be open to receiving encouragement, and allow others to contribute to your journey. Their support can have a profound impact on your personal and professional growth, and together, you can achieve remarkable things. *Simply allow a strong self-belief and external encouragement from others to validate you and spur you on to keep going.*

This is modeled in the biblical story of the Apostle Paul and his perpetual encourager, Barnabas. Paul had been literally knocked off his horse, interrupting his mission entirely. He found himself blind, in the home of a stranger, and without a clear vision for the future. The disciples initially rejected him. They were afraid of him because his original mission involved killing them and those associated with them. Barnabas, whose name means encourager, connected with Apostle Paul, took him under his wing, and mentored him. Apostle Paul ultimately passed Barnabas in the ministry. So, despite the fact that Barnabas was an established leader, he accepted Apostle Paul, and his ongoing encouragement led Apostle Paul to become one of the most influential leaders to ever live, writing two-thirds of the New Testament!

Through his courageous acceptance and decision to encourage, he exposed Apostle Paul to possibilities he may not have been aware of and opportunities he didn't previously consider. Those new possibilities may have been lodged deep within his subconscious, and a fresh set of eyes were what he needed to pull them to the forefront of it all. The end result is that Barnabas' encouragement validated him and caused Apostle Paul to press on! If you have encountered a setback, it's only a setup for your comeback. Look for the encourager that God has brought into your life.

For you, it may be determining the direction of your job, determining how to communicate your uniqueness, identifying ways to obtain this opportunity, and so forth. It is so empowering to be validated.

This type of encouragement can also be contagious and spread to all those around you. This happens because receiving encouragement feels good, which, in turn, motivates you to give encouragement to others, so they can feel the same way. Then, those individuals go through the same process as you did, and before you know it, everyone on your team is sharing words of encouragement. A positive and encouraging culture is established among the team, and it's all because of your commitment to being a perpetual encourager.

5 Methods of Encouragement

Most people subscribe to the notion that the majority of what you communicate has little correlation to the actual words being said. Instead, communication primarily consists of body language, tone, and non-verbal expressions. Effective encouragement follows this same logic and goes beyond mere verbal affirmations and extends into the realm of non-verbal cues and actions. When we encourage someone, we are not just speaking words of support, but we are also conveying our belief in their abilities and showing them that we are there for them.

Body language plays a crucial role in expressing encouragement. A simple smile, a nod of approval, or a pat on the back can communicate volumes of encouragement without uttering a single word. These non-verbal cues create a positive and welcoming environment, making the recipient feel acknowledged and valued.

Tone of voice is another essential element of effective encouragement. When we speak with a warm and enthusiastic tone, our words become more impactful and uplifting. A monotone or disinterested voice can convey a lack of genuine encouragement, whereas an enthusiastic and sincere tone can inspire and motivate others.

Furthermore, actions speak louder than words when it comes to encouragement. Taking the time to listen attentively, offering help, or providing constructive feedback can show genuine support and encouragement. Actions demonstrate our commitment to someone's growth and success, reinforcing the belief that they are capable and deserving of encouragement.

While kind words are valuable, true encouragement encompasses much more. Body language, tone of voice, and non-verbal expressions are essential components of effective encouragement. By recognizing the significance of these factors, we can offer genuine encouragement that uplifts and empowers others.

5 Methods of Encouragement:

1) *Encourage others with your eyes.* Never undervalue eye contact. Consider the folks you know who seem to maintain constant eye contact with you during conversation. What are your thoughts about them? Do you feel like they believe in you and support you? Do they appear to be more concerned about the things you're going through?

When someone maintains constant eye contact during a conversation, it can have a significant impact on how we perceive them. Here are a few thoughts about individuals who engage in consistent eye contact:

1. Trust and belief: People who maintain eye contact often come across as trustworthy and confident. Their gaze suggests that they believe in what you are saying and that they have faith in your abilities. This can boost your confidence and make you feel supported.

2. Active listening: Eye contact is a sign of active listening and genuine interest. When someone maintains eye contact, it shows that they are fully present in the

conversation and focused on understanding your thoughts and emotions. This can make you feel valued and heard.

3. Empathy and concern: Constant eye contact can also convey empathy and concern for your well-being. It indicates that the person is genuinely interested in your experiences and wants to understand what you're going through. This can create a sense of comfort and reassurance.

4. Connection and engagement: Eye contact fosters a deeper sense of connection and engagement between individuals. It can enhance the quality of the conversation, making it more meaningful and intimate. This can help in building stronger relationships and fostering open and effective communication.

Most of us have positive thoughts about those who maintain eye contact with us. We often describe these people as supportive, attentive, and concerned. This illustrates the potency of good eye contact. Perhaps these individuals may never use their words to encourage you, but their presence and eye contact have served their own purpose in this regard.

However, it is important to note that the interpretation of eye contact may vary among individuals and across diverse cultures. Some people may find prolonged eye contact uncomfortable, while others may perceive it positively. It's essential to consider individual preferences and cultural norms when assessing the impact of eye contact on delivering effective encouragement.

I host "The Martin Houston Show" and open every show with, "Today is a day that the Lord has made, so let's rejoice and be glad in it. Take some time to notice (see them) someone, serve someone, love someone. Be the difference you want to see in the world today." Noticing someone through attentive eye contact will lead to unexpected opportunities as an encourager, even when there are no words being exchanged. It reminds me of one of my favorite scriptures, where it emphasizes that God's eyes will be open (He never sleeps) indicating a special focus in His gaze upon us.

Now My eyes will be open and My ears attentive to the prayers offered in this place. 2 Chronicles 7:15

2) *Encourage through facial expressions.* A smile is an excellent motivator and encourager. It communicates to people that they are safe. It communicates to people that what they are doing is okay, and that they should keep going.

"Let us always meet each other with a smile, for the smile is the beginning of love." – Mother Teresa

A smile is a powerful non-verbal form of communication that can have a positive impact on individuals. Here are a few reasons why a smile can be an excellent motivator and encourager:

1. Creates a positive atmosphere: A smile can instantly brighten up a room and create a welcoming and friendly environment. When people feel comfortable and safe, they are more likely to be motivated to engage and participate in activities.

2. Boosts morale and confidence: Seeing someone smile can be uplifting and reassuring. It gives individuals a sense of acknowledgment and appreciation for their efforts, which can

boost their morale and confidence. This, in turn, encourages them to continue their work with enthusiasm.

3. Fosters connection and teamwork: A smile can help build connections and foster teamwork among individuals. It signals a sense of camaraderie and support, making people feel that they are part of a united group working towards a common goal. This can encourage individuals to collaborate and support each other.

4. Reduces stress and anxiety: Smiling releases endorphins, which are natural mood boosters. When people feel stressed or anxious, a smile can help alleviate their negative emotions and create a more relaxed and positive mindset. This can encourage individuals to approach challenges with a clearer and calmer perspective.

5. Acts as a form of encouragement: A smile can serve as a silent form of encouragement. It shows individuals that their efforts are recognized and appreciated, motivating them to continue their endeavors. It also communicates to them that they are not alone and that others believe in their abilities.

A smile can be a powerful motivator and encourager as it creates a positive atmosphere, boosts morale, fosters connections, reduces stress, and acts as a form of silent encouragement. So, let's remember to share our smiles and spread positivity to inspire and motivate those around us!

For some people, smiling comes effortlessly, while others must work at it. In either case, there are almost certainly more moments and settings in which you can show off your pearly whites. Smiling is contagious, and almost always triggers an equal response. When you smile, you encourage others and feel better yourself. Another win-win!

4 Health Benefits of Smiling:

It's generally believed that smiling can have several health benefits.

Here's a bit more detail on each:

1. **Lowers blood pressure:**
   Smiling and laughing are thought to help reduce the body's stress response, which can, in turn, lower blood pressure. When you smile, endorphins are released, and these natural feel-good chemicals can help relax the body.

2. **Puts you in a better mood:**
   Smiling is often said to trigger the release of neurotransmitters like dopamine and serotonin in the brain, which are associated with feelings of happiness and well-being. This can help improve your mood and overall outlook on life.

3. **Relieves stress:**
   Smiling and laughter can help reduce the level of stress hormones like cortisol in the body. By doing so, smiling may contribute to a more relaxed and less stressed state of mind.

4. **Strengthens your immune system:**
   Some studies have suggested that the act of smiling and the positive emotions it generates might have a positive impact on the immune system. However, the direct link between smiling and immune system function is still an area of ongoing research.

While the precise health benefits of smiling may vary from person to person and the scientific evidence supporting these claims isn't definitive, many people find that smiling and laughter can indeed have positive effects on their well-being.

3) *Encourage with your feet.*

Encouragement can take the form of simply being there for somebody and being present for the things they are going through. Attend a meeting that someone has invited you to, even if you are confident they can manage it on their own. Attend a baseball game or an after-hours function to support those on your team.

By showing up and being present, you are sending a message that you value and support the person or team. This can have a positive impact on their motivation and confidence. Additionally, when you attend events or meetings, you might have the opportunity to offer words of encouragement or praise, further boosting their spirits.

In addition to physically attending events, you can also encourage others with your feet by taking action. Offer to help out with tasks or projects that may be overwhelming for someone. By lending a hand, you are showing your support and willingness to assist, which can be incredibly encouraging. By being present and attentive, you can provide the emotional support that someone may need.

Ultimately, encouraging others with your feet means actively showing up, taking action, and being present for the people and situations that matter to them. Your physical presence and support can have a significant impact on their motivation, confidence, and overall well-being.

> *Application: Walk through the crowd slowly and take time to notice them. The CEO of Alabama One, Bill Wells, models this trait better than any leader I've ever seen. Not only is he present at a multitude of functions and meetings, but he is also actively engaged, which is encouraging to those hosting and leading the event.*

Your presence and attention can be an extremely effective motivator and form of encouragement. Recognize that your support, words, body language, and so on can all be encouraging on their own, but your presence can elevate the encouragement to the next level. If you are present, then you can proactively notice the beneficial things your team members are doing, allowing you to immediately respond with the appropriate level of encouragement.

4) *Encourage with your head.*
If all you notice are the incorrect things people are doing, it becomes incredibly difficult to maintain an optimistic mindset. The most significant obstacle that some of us must overcome to be more encouraging is making an intentional note of the positive things rather than the negative. Our mindset must be positive because if we have a positive mindset, then we will notice the positive things.

Remember, encouragement is a powerful tool that can uplift others and inspire them to reach their full potential. By focusing on the positive aspects of people's actions and achievements, you will not only boost their confidence but also cultivate a more optimistic outlook for them.

Instead of solely pointing out mistakes or flaws, challenge yourself to actively seek out and acknowledge the things that individuals are doing right. It may be a small step forward, an act of kindness, or a display of resilience. By celebrating these positive moments, you will create an environment that fosters growth, motivation, and a sense of accomplishment.

Remember, a positive mindset is contagious. When you choose to see the good in others and encourage them with genuine enthusiasm, it not only benefits them but also contributes to your own well-being. It allows you to focus on progress rather than perfection, and to appreciate the effort and dedication that goes into every endeavor.

So, make a conscious effort to encourage with your head. Train yourself to see the positive, to uplift others, and to foster an environment of optimism and growth. You can make a difference by spreading encouragement and empowering those around you to believe in themselves.

5) *Encourage with your mouth*.
Aside from encouraging with our physical attributes and the right mindset, it is important, of course, that we also encourage with our words. We are all capable of encouraging with our words.

Use your words to encourage:

1. Be specific: Instead of saying, "Good job," try saying, "Great job on completing that task on time and exceeding expectations." By being specific, you show that you are paying attention and appreciate their efforts.

2. Use positive language: Focus on the positive aspects of their work or actions. Instead of criticizing what they did wrong, highlight what they did right. For example, say, "I really appreciate your attention to detail" instead of "You made fewer mistakes this time."

3. Show genuine appreciation: Take the time to sincerely express your gratitude and acknowledge the individual's efforts. Let them know that their work is valued and makes a difference. This can boost their morale and motivation.

4. Offer constructive feedback: Encouragement doesn't always mean only praising someone. It can also involve giving helpful suggestions for improvement. Frame your feedback in a positive and supportive manner, highlighting areas for growth rather than pointing out flaws.

5. Be a cheerleader: Use your words to inspire and motivate. Share words of encouragement and remind the person of their strengths and abilities. Let them know that you believe in their potential and that you are there to support them.

Remember, the way we communicate can have a significant impact on others. By choosing to encourage with our words, we can create a positive and uplifting environment that promotes growth and success.

So, make your statements precise and specific; avoid general statements that do not pinpoint the exact action you are trying to acknowledge and encourage. Demonstrate to the individual how much you value them. Inform them of the value their contribution adds to the team. Remember, it's said that *the power of life and death is in your tongue!* So, use your words to encourage rather than tear down!

"Do not let any unwholesome talk come out of your mouths, but only what is helpful for building others up according to their needs, that it may benefit those who listen." - Eph 4:29

It's Game Time

Now, it's important we implement the lessons taught so far.

Application Task:
First, create an index card with these five methods of encouragement listed and carry it with you each day. Work on implementing these methods.

Refer to the card as a reminder to continue employing these methods to increase and enhance your encouragement.

You'll be amazed at the changes you'll notice in individuals around you and in your own life. You have the ability to do this, so let's go encourage.

Many people confuse encouragement with praise. Praise can be an extremely helpful tool to implement in your leadership style and can mimic the discipline of encouragement. Misguided praise, on the other hand, can create a whole list of complications, especially for parents and children. Let's see what we can learn about the differences between these concepts. This is especially important for us as parents—especially helicopter and lawnmower parents—don't want our children to go through anything difficult, false praise has evolved into a harmful instrument that we employ in today's culture.

So more than ever, it is critically important that we know how to differentiate between praise and encouragement. So, let's exam how to differentiate between praise and encouragement.

Encouragement is defined as *instilling a sense of courage.*

If done correctly, encouragement consistently teaches us to:

- Develop an internal gauge for self-assessment.

- Determine what is significant.
- Spend less time inquiring about what others (the rest of the world) thinks about us.

Encouragement:

- is a statement directed to an individual.
- is an act of recognition.
- is focused on effort, progress, and improvement rather than just results; it can be given at any moment in time, without any specific targets being met or exceptions being made.
- contributes to the development of self-esteem.

Example of Encouragement: I know that you have struggled to complete the project, but I believe in you, so don't give up.

Praise:

- is a judgment or statement about a person.
- tends to focus on the finished result or outcome with a special emphasis on winners and losers.
- can lead people to become reliant on what others think.

Example of Praise: I'm so proud of you for getting an A on the test; you are such a good student.

The important distinction between these two concepts is that praise leans toward a final judgment, whereas encouragement simply offers recognition of a status (good or bad) at any given moment in time.

Encouragement entails believing in and respecting people for who they are and who they can become. It's not just about what they've already done. It also serves to acknowledge their future potential.

Be an encourager. Regular encouragement will help you develop a greater sense of interest in people and their unique journeys. You will become a bigger part of people's lives as a result.

An encourager:

- Accepts others in their natural state and doesn't try to fundamentally change them.

- Communicates hope and faith instead of just expectations and standards.
- Concentrates on the positives and encourages through negatives.
- Considers effort and progress.

Encouragement is oxygen for the soul! Wouldn't it be nice if we all encouraged one another? Just think how it makes you feel when coworkers, leaders, or managers compliment you on your effort, your attitude, and your behavior!

Encouragement functions like a spinning top. When we wind up the toy, it spins in circles and maintains its balance. However, as the top winds down, it begins to wobble from side to side aimlessly, and becomes incredibly unstable and imbalanced.

We, as human beings, are quite similar. We have balance and direction when our actions are validated through encouragement, but without that validating encouragement, our decisions can become shaky, and we can wobble from goal to goal, often never hitting our intended aim.

Encouragement has the potential to significantly change someone's life. Here is a story of how one brief moment of encouragement changed a young man's journey. This young man worked at his job proudly, but he felt like he could do more. He felt like he wasn't reaching his full potential.

He worked at what was perceived to be a lowly job of putting stamps on vouchers that would eventually be mailed out. He despised that job but couldn't leave because he was lacking any perceived marketable abilities. One day, the organization's director strolled by his desk and asked, "How do you like your job?" He told the director that he believed he could be better and could do better work; he wanted to be challenged more.

His director acknowledged and supported his statement with encouragement. She looked into his eyes, smiled, and said, "You are brighter than your current work and you can improve your circumstances. All that is required of you is to attend college."

The young man paused for a moment and absorbed her words of encouragement. It was clear that she offered him support and the motivation that he needed at that moment of doubt. Fast-forward 4 years later: The young man graduated from college and landed his dream job. Those few encouraging words gave him the nudge and a little direction on how he could change the course of his life. With few exceptions, words of encouragement have the tremendous power to push people forward.

At Alabama One, my current employer at the time of authoring this book, we have several testimonies from individuals who have moved from teller to branch manager, from part-time teller to training specialist, and from teller to processor. These are just a few examples of team members who were encouraged to succeed in their current role, but also challenged to equip themselves to pursue other opportunities. I have personally experienced the power of encouragement to push forward, as I have had numerous encounters of encouragement that kept me fully engaged until opportunities to pursue different roles and responsibilities came my way. My personal journey has equipped, empowered, and encouraged me to be an encourager of others along my journey. I find it extremely rewarding to encourage others to press on and continue to grow and develop in their current role but keep their eyes on future opportunities.

There is a powerful benefit of encouragement that I call the boomerang effect. It is true that when we uplift and support others, it often encourages them to do the same for us in return. By offering genuine and heartfelt encouragement, we create a positive and uplifting environment that fosters growth and happiness.

Being authentic and sincere in our encouragement is crucial. People can easily sense when someone is being insincere or sarcastic, and it can have a negative impact instead of being uplifting. When our words come from the heart, they carry much more meaning and have a greater impact on the receiver.

It's important to make a habit of encouraging others regularly, rather than just when we feel like it. Opportunities to encourage others arise constantly, and by making a conscious effort to seize those opportunities, we can create a culture of support and positivity. Encouragement is not something that should be reserved for special occasions; it should be a constant presence in our interactions with others.

Understanding the boomerang effect of encouragement can inspire more people to uplift and support others. By being authentic, sincere, and consistently offering encouragement, we can create a positive cycle of support that benefits everyone involved.

Setting goals is crucial for several reasons. Firstly, clear goals provide direction and focus. They give individuals and organizations a sense of purpose and help them stay on track towards their desired outcomes. Without goals, we may wander aimlessly and make little progress towards our objectives.

Secondly, goals provide a means of measuring progress. By setting specific and measurable goals, individuals and organizations can track their achievements and identify areas for improvement. This allows for better decision-making and resource allocation.

Thirdly, goals promote accountability. When goals are made public, individuals and teams are more likely to take ownership of their responsibilities. They become accountable to themselves and others, which enhances motivation and commitment to achieving the desired results.

Moreover, setting goals helps prioritize tasks and allocate resources effectively. By clearly defining what needs to be accomplished, individuals and organizations can identify the most important and urgent tasks. This enables efficient use of time, energy, and resources towards achieving desired outcomes.

Lastly, setting goals fosters teamwork and alignment. When goals are shared and communicated, it ensures that everyone is working towards a common purpose. This promotes collaboration, cooperation, and synergy among team members, leading to improved productivity and overall organizational success.

Overall, setting goals is crucial for organizational growth, advancement, and professional success. It provides direction, measurement, accountability, prioritization, and alignment. By setting S.M.A.R.T. goals and making them public, individuals and organizations can set themselves up for success and ensure everyone is working towards the same objectives.

S.M.A.R.T. goals are a framework for setting objectives that are specific, measurable, attainable, relevant, and timely. Let's break down each component:

1. Specific: A goal should be clear and well-defined. It should answer the questions: What do I want to accomplish? Why is it important? Who is involved? Where will it happen? This specificity provides clarity and focus.

2. Measurable: A goal should have a way to measure progress and determine whether it has been achieved. It should answer the questions: How much? How many? How will I know when it is accomplished? This helps track progress and provides motivation.

3. Attainable: A goal should be realistic and achievable. It should be challenging enough to inspire growth and effort but not so unrealistic that it becomes demotivating. It should answer the question: Is it possible to achieve this goal based on my current resources and circumstances?

4. Relevant: A goal should be aligned with the broader objectives and mission. It should be meaningful and have

a direct impact on the individual or organization. It should answer the question: Does this goal matter and contribute to overall success?

5. Timely: A goal should have a specific timeframe or deadline. It should answer the question: When will I achieve this goal? This creates a sense of urgency and helps prioritize actions.

By incorporating these elements into goal setting, individuals and organizations increase the likelihood of success. S.M.A.R.T. goals provide a structured approach that ensures goals are specific, measurable, attainable, relevant, and timely, leading to better focus, motivation, and progress.

While recording your goals, identify what everyone is expected to contribute. These objectives will act as your road map to success. After ensuring that everyone on the team knows and values their position in the game plan, it's time to get started. It is important to maintain motivation among **all** stakeholders to accomplish your stated objectives. Learning how to succeed in business is not the sole responsibility of a single individual; it is a collaborative endeavor.

6 Steps to help motivate team members to meet goals:

1) *Regularly re-evaluating the goals* helps motivate team members by creating a sense of progress and growth. It allows them to see their accomplishments and how far they have come, which can boost their motivation to continue working towards the goals. Additionally, re-evaluating goals helps ensure that they are realistic and aligned with the team's current needs and resources, which can increase team members' confidence in achieving them.

2) *Establishing a culture that values progress* motivates team members by creating an environment where their efforts and achievements are recognized and celebrated. When progress is valued, team members feel appreciated and motivated to continue working towards the goals. It also fosters a sense of camaraderie and healthy

competition among team members, which can further drive their motivation to meet the goals.

3) *Regularly providing feedback* motivates team members by giving them a clear understanding of their performance and areas for improvement. Positive feedback acknowledges their efforts and achievements, reinforcing their motivation. Constructive feedback helps them identify areas where they can grow and develop, providing them with a roadmap to meet the goals. When team members receive regular feedback, they feel supported and valued, which can increase their motivation to meet the goals.

4) *Encouraging innovation* motivates team members by empowering them to think creatively and find innovative solutions to challenges. When team members are encouraged to innovate, they feel a sense of ownership and pride in their work. This can increase their motivation as they see the impact of their ideas and contributions on the team's progress towards the goals. Encouraging innovation also fosters a culture of continuous

improvement and learning, which can further motivate team members to meet the goals.

5) *Encouraging through mistakes* motivates team members by creating a safe and supportive environment where they are not afraid to take risks and make mistakes. When team members know that mistakes are seen as learning opportunities rather than failures, they are more likely to experiment, try innovative approaches, and push their boundaries. This can lead to increased motivation as they learn from their mistakes and grow professionally, ultimately contributing to the team's ability to meet the goals.

6) *Increase an individual's potential by* providing them with opportunities for growth and development. When team members feel that their potential is recognized and nurtured, they are more motivated to work towards the goals. This can be done through training programs, mentoring, or assigning challenging tasks that allow team members to stretch their skills and abilities. By investing in their development, team members feel valued and are more likely to be motivated to meet the goals.

By recognizing and understanding each team member's unique skills, abilities, and professional background, you can tailor your approach to effectively motivate and encourage them to achieve their goals. This personalized approach acknowledges that individuals have different strengths and weaknesses, and it allows you to provide the necessary support and guidance for each team member to succeed.

When you personalize your approach, you show that you value and respect each team member as an individual, which fosters a positive and inclusive team culture. This, in turn, creates a supportive environment where team members feel empowered and motivated to work towards their goals.

Another benefit of personalizing your approach is that it helps you identify the specific strategies and methods that resonate with each team member. Some individuals may respond well to visual aids and step-by-step instructions, while others may prefer more hands-on learning experiences. By understanding these preferences, you can adapt your communication and coaching style to maximize their engagement and productivity.

Additionally, personalizing your approach allows you to identify any potential challenges or barriers that may hinder a team member's progress towards their goals. By addressing these issues early on and providing the necessary resources and support, you can help them overcome obstacles and stay on track.

Overall, personalizing your approach to goal setting and achievement is crucial for individual and team success. It enables you to leverage each team member's unique strengths, address their individual needs and preferences, and create a supportive and inclusive environment that fosters growth and achievement.

Everyone—whether they're a CEO, mother, father, child, employee, professional athlete, or performer—requires encouragement at some point. This goes for the high achievers or the cellar dwellers!

Encouragement plays a vital role in our lives, regardless of our roles or achievements. Here are a few reasons why everyone needs encouragement:

1. Boosting of Confidence: Encouragement can provide a much-needed confidence boost. It reminds individuals of their abilities and strengths, helping them believe in themselves and their potential. This is crucial for anyone striving to achieve their goals, whether it's a CEO leading a company or a child learning new skills.

2. Overcoming Challenges: Life is filled with challenges, and encouragement can be the fuel that keeps us going. When faced with obstacles or setbacks, a supportive word or gesture can motivate individuals to persevere and find solutions. It helps them maintain a positive mindset and not give up easily.

3. Building Resilience: Encouragement fosters resilience, enabling individuals to bounce back from failures or disappointments. It teaches them to view setbacks as learning experiences rather than reasons to quit. This resilience is valuable for everyone, from professional athletes facing defeats to employees dealing with setbacks in their careers.

4. Nurturing Creativity: Encouragement stimulates creativity and innovation. By providing positive feedback and support, individuals feel more comfortable taking risks and exploring new ideas. This applies to professionals in creative fields, such as performers or artists, as well as anyone seeking innovative solutions in their personal or professional lives.

5. Strengthening Relationships: Encouragement strengthens relationships and fosters a sense of belonging. Whether it's a parent encouraging their child, a colleague supporting a coworker, or a friend cheering on another friend, these acts of encouragement create a bond and foster a positive environment. It helps individuals feel

valued, appreciated, and motivated to support others in return.

6. Maintaining Mental Health: Encouragement plays an essential role in maintaining mental well-being. It can provide emotional support, reduce stress, and combat feelings of self-doubt or loneliness. This applies to people in all walks of life, as everyone faces challenges and moments of vulnerability.

Encouragement is a universal need that transcends age, occupation, or achievements. It has the power to motivate, uplift, and support individuals in their personal and professional endeavors. So, let's remember to offer encouragement to others and seek and receive it ourselves when needed.

Reminder: Encouragement is a term that refers to the act of inspiring, inciting, cultivating, stimulating, and instilling courage with hope attached. As many of us recall from childhood, we occasionally required encouragement to complete a chore. This is because we tend to borrow motivation from words of encouragement when our personal motivation is running low.

As adults, our circumstances may have changed, but the human condition of requiring that extra boost of mojo has remained the same. At some point, we all require some level of encouragement. Whatever your life's mission is, and regardless of whether you work in healthcare, education, business, criminal justice, ministry, or any of the other tens of thousands of fields, you should make it your priority to encourage others.

Encouragement has the power to uplift, motivate, and inspire. It can make someone's day, boost their confidence, and provide them with the support they need in tough times. By withholding encouragement, we deny others the chance to experience these positive effects.

When we refrain from providing encouragement, we fail to seize the chance to make a positive impact in someone's life. Like an unoccupied seat on a plane during takeoff, our silence or hesitation creates an empty space that could have been filled.

Furthermore, the potential influence of encouragement dwindles as time passes. Postponing the expression of our encouraging words diminishes their effectiveness and significance. Individuals require encouragement in the present moment, especially when they are confronted with obstacles or pursuing their goals. By withholding it, we deprive them of the timely upliftment they may greatly require.

Instead of hoarding or denying encouragement, let us embrace a mindset of generosity and empathy. Let us seize every opportunity to offer kind words, support, and motivation. By doing so, we create a ripple effect of positivity that can uplift not only individuals but also our communities and society as a whole.

Encouragement holds immense power, yet we often underestimate its impact. A kind word, a simple gesture, or a heartfelt note can make all the difference in someone's day, or even their life. It costs us nothing to offer encouragement, yet its value is immeasurable.

We all face challenges and hardships at various points in our lives. In those moments, a little encouragement can be the spark that keeps us going. It can reignite our motivation, restore our faith, and remind us that we are not alone in our struggles. By sharing encouragement, we become a source of strength for others, helping them navigate challenging times with a renewed sense of purpose.

Opportunities to offer encouragement may present themselves unexpectedly, in the most ordinary of situations. It could be a coworker grappling with a demanding project, a friend facing personal setbacks, or a stranger dealing with their own battles. By keeping our eyes open and our hearts receptive, we can seize these chances to make a positive impact.

Encouragement is not confined to grand gestures or eloquent speeches. It can be as simple as offering a genuine compliment, lending a listening ear, or expressing belief in someone's abilities. Sometimes, all it takes is a smile, a warm embrace, or a reassuring pat on the back. These small acts of encouragement can create a ripple effect, spreading positivity and inspiration to those around us.

When we offer encouragement freely and generously, we create a supportive community where people feel valued, understood, and empowered. We become beacons of hope, lighting the way for those who may be lost in the darkness of self-doubt or despair. Our words and actions can serve as catalysts for change, igniting a fire within others that propels them forward on their journey.

It is important to remember that encouragement is perishable. Its impact diminishes if left unspoken or withheld. We must not let fear, indifference, or busyness prevent us from sharing words of encouragement with those who need them most. In a world that can often feel cold and discouraging, our acts of kindness and support have the potential to create lasting positive change.

So, let us be mindful of the opportunities that arise each day to offer encouragement. Let us give the gift of encouragement and be generous with our words, gestures, and support. Together, we can create a world where encouragement is abundant, where hope and inspiration thrive, and where everyone feels empowered to overcome their challenges.

Encouragement holds immense power to uplift and inspire both the recipient and the giver. It can create a ripple effect of positivity, spreading through individuals and communities. Never underestimate the impact of your supportive words on another human being. Know that your words of support can provide the strength and motivation needed for someone to overcome obstacles and pursue their goals. By acknowledging someone's efforts and believing in their potential, you can ignite a sense of confidence and self-belief that can push them forward.

Moreover, the act of encouraging others can also have a profound impact on your own well-being. When we uplift and inspire others, we experience a sense of fulfillment and joy. It reminds us of the interconnectedness of humanity and our ability to make a positive difference in the lives of others. By sharing encouragement, we cultivate a culture of kindness, empathy, and support, creating a more compassionate world for everyone.

It is essential to recognize that you have the power to influence others' lives, regardless of the magnitude or duration of your interaction. A kind word, a genuine compliment, or a simple gesture of encouragement can leave a lasting impression on someone's heart. You never know what battles someone may be fighting internally, and your encouraging words may be the lifeline they need to keep going.

Furthermore, encouragement is a gift that comes at no cost to you. It requires only a moment of your time and the willingness to uplift another person. By giving encouragement freely, you contribute to the well-being and happiness of those around you. The impact of your words may be immeasurable, and the positive change they create can be priceless.

So, let us never underestimate the power of our supportive words. Let us be mindful of the influence we have on others and seize every opportunity to encourage those we meet. By doing so, we can create a world where kindness, encouragement, and compassion are valued and cherished. Remember, your words have the power to shape destinies, and through encouragement, you can make a difference in someone's life, one uplifting word at a time.

Indeed, encouragement is truly a gift and the act of giving and receiving encouragement is a reciprocal and mutually beneficial process. It is crucial to acknowledge and appreciate the encouragement we receive from others, as it reflects their belief in our abilities and potential. By valuing their support, we validate their faith in us and reinforce the positive impact of their words.

At the same time, we must recognize our own worth and the significance of our encouragement towards others. Each person possesses unique qualities, perspectives, and strengths that make their encouragement invaluable.

That being said, it is essential to approach encouragement with sincerity and intentionality. Genuine and deliberate encouragement goes beyond empty praise or flattery. It involves recognizing and acknowledging the efforts, progress, and achievements of others. By offering specific and heartfelt encouragement, we demonstrate that we see and appreciate their hard work and dedication.

It is a misconception that successful individuals do not need encouragement. In reality, everyone benefits from encouragement, regardless of their accomplishments or status. Successful people often face tremendous pressure and expectations, and your support can serve as a source of motivation and inspiration. By providing encouragement, you can help them maintain their commitment and drive, knowing that their efforts are recognized and valued.

Remember, encouragement is not limited to grand gestures or extravagant displays. It can be as simple as a kind word, a genuine compliment, or a thoughtful gesture. By consistently seeking ways to uplift and encourage others, we foster a culture of positivity, support, and growth.

Embrace the gift of encouragement and give and receive it graciously. Your words hold the power to empower and inspire others, and their words have the potential to uplift and motivate you. Let us all appreciate the significance of encouragement, both in our own lives and in the lives of those around us. Together, we can create a world where encouragement is cherished and celebrated, contributing to the well-being and success of all.

Tip: Encouragement is free! Give it away! Your act of encouragement has the potential to positively impact millions. It can become the gift that keeps on giving!

The *Pay It Forward* project estimated that if three acts of kindness were given away by one person and repeated daily by each subsequent person, 4,787,969 lives would be impacted in only 2 weeks.

My challenge to you is this: By the end of today, encourage at least 3 individuals and request that they do the same for 3 others. Then, ask them to challenge those 3 to keep it going and so on and so forth. I guarantee you will gain confidence and a higher sense of self-worth as a result.

My Personal Testimony: How Encouragement is a Gift

I had a really good childhood and was surrounded by many encouragers along the way to adulthood. My mom was my first and most important encourager, both in her words and the way she led by example. She was the first person to show (encourage) me the value of hard-work and the reward that came along with it. Today, my life is filled with many cheerleaders (encouragers), including my wife! She has been and remains my biggest cheerleader. If it weren't for her, I'm sure I would not have achieved most of the things I have achieved thus far. Her encouragement has been one of the greatest gifts I've ever received. Now, I also pride myself on being a cheerleader (a gift giver) for my family, friends, coworkers, and acquaintances.

My Personal Mission Statement: May the lives of those around me and the people whom I meet and interact with in life be better off after having met me than they would have been otherwise.

My goal is to positively impact the lives of others by fostering meaningful connections, providing support, and inspiring growth, so that they may flourish and achieve their full potential.

Adopting this personal mission statement forces me to notice, serve, and love people without any promise of receiving anything in return, which is why I call encouragement a gift. My mom, wife, family, and friends have all given me the gift of encouragement, while also receiving this gift from me, with no expectation of getting something in return and with no strings attached. My goal in sharing this information is to testify that being a perpetual encourager is beneficial and effective, and is, in fact, foundational to becoming an empowered leader.

Since I've made an effort to surround myself with perpetual encouragers, I've noticed a few shared characteristics amongst those who fall into the perpetual encourager category.

Perpetual encouragers:

A perpetual encourager is a person who believes that the glass is half full—or better yet, it is someone who believes that the glass has exactly the amount of liquid needed for the task at hand.

Traits of Perpetual Encouragers:

1. Positivity: A perpetual encourager always maintains a positive outlook and sees the good in people and situations. They focus on the strengths and achievements of others rather than dwelling on their weaknesses or failures.

2. Empathy: They have the ability to understand and share the feelings of others. A perpetual encourager can put themselves in someone else's shoes, offering comfort and support when needed.

3. Active Listening: They listen attentively and engage in meaningful conversations. A perpetual encourager pays close attention to others, understanding their needs and concerns, and offers words of encouragement and support based on what they have heard.

4. Genuine Care: They genuinely care about the well-being and success of others. A perpetual encourager goes beyond just offering empty words of encouragement. They take the time to understand the goals and dreams of others and provide guidance and support to help them achieve their aspirations.

5. Motivation: They inspire and motivate others to reach their full potential. A perpetual encourager understands the importance of motivation and uses their words and actions to uplift and inspire those around them.
6. Resilience: They have a resilient spirit, bouncing back from setbacks and inspiring others to do the same. A

perpetual encourager doesn't let their own challenges hinder their ability to uplift and encourage others.

7. Authenticity: They are genuine and authentic in their encouragement. A perpetual encourager believes in the power of authenticity and speaks from the heart, providing sincere and meaningful words of encouragement to others.

8. Lead by Example: A perpetual encourager leads by setting an example for others to follow. They don't just preach, but actively engage in the actions they promote. Whether they are experienced or just starting out, these individuals hold themselves and others to a higher standard. They are willing to take risks and motivate others to join them in the journey or inspire them to embark on their own path of growth and success.

9. Listen Attentively: Perpetual encouragers understand that encouraging does not simply mean telling others to "get themselves up" or "get over it." They are receptive and attentive. They want to know and understand the person. They also want to make sure

that their encouragement aligns with the individual's goals and mission, rather than simply fulfilling what the leader expects of them. For example, when a child is a good athlete and equally talented in arts, a perpetual encourager will talk to the child and determine their preferred course of action. Then, they will encourage them to pursue this course of action, considering their abilities, skills, and life experiences to inform the situation. The advice you provide may contradict what the child wants to hear, but it will be informed and based on what is perceived to be the best path to pursue.

10. Avoid Clichés: A perpetual encourager goes beyond clichés. By actively listening to others, they naturally avoid using generic phrases like "You can do it!" or "Let go of your fear!" Although there is nothing wrong with those phrases when used sincerely and authentically. They recognize that true encouragement requires a deeper understanding of the individual and their unique circumstances. Instead, they provide personalized and specific words of support that are tailored to the person they are interacting with. This

approach ensures that their encouragement is sincere, authentic, and meaningful, making a positive impact on the recipient's unique situation.

11. Recognize Self-Doubt and Condemnation, but Don't Build a House There: Perpetual encouragers are aware of the presence of self-doubt and self-condemnation in themselves and others. These voices often tell us that we cannot or should not pursue certain endeavors, predicting failure or embarrassment if we try. However, perpetual encouragers do not let these voices define them or others. Instead, they acknowledge the existence of these thoughts and emotions but do not dwell on them. They understand that these voices gain power through acceptance, so they actively reject them. Regardless of how persistent or loud these voices may be, perpetual encouragers refuse to give in to them or let them negatively impact their actions or the actions of those they support. Look for the positive in every situation, and spin it into a lesson.

12. Prosper in All Situations: A perpetual encourager recognizes that even with wisdom and experience, everyone can make choices that may not seem wise. In

such moments, the role of a perpetual encourager becomes invaluable for both them and the individuals they guide. Their aim is to uplift others' spirits and highlight the positive aspects of a situation, including the lessons that can be learned from any mistakes, errors, or failures. They embrace the opportunity to transform a negative experience into a positive one, using it as a chance for growth and improvement. By focusing on the lessons that can be derived from both positive and negative situations, perpetual encouragers inspire resilience and a positive mindset among those they support.

13. Prophetic (forward thinking) in Their Outlook: Perpetual encouragers possess a prophetic and forward-thinking outlook. They have the ability to see beyond the present circumstances and envision the potential of a person or situation. Instead of focusing on current limitations or shortcomings, they use their gift of encouragement to instill hope and courage. They recognize the inner potential within individuals and inspire them to strive towards that higher version of themselves. Perpetual encouragers see the inherent

greatness in people, rather than dwelling on temporary setbacks or mistakes. They have the ability to turn challenges into opportunities and find the positive in any situation. As a perpetual encourager, it is important to continue uplifting others, even when it may seem challenging. Your ability to see the best in people and situations can truly make a difference and turn adversity into triumph.

14. Understands that Growth and Development is a Journey: Perpetual encouragers understand that growth and development are ongoing journeys. They recognize that team members need the opportunity and support to progress and improve. They understand that no one becomes their best self-overnight and that it takes time and effort to develop skills and abilities. Perpetual encouragers provide the necessary coaching, guidance, and resources to help team members grow and reach their full potential. They celebrate small victories along the way and understand that setbacks and mistakes are part of the learning process. Instead of focusing on perfection, perpetual encouragers emphasize progress and

continuous improvement. They create a nurturing and supportive environment where team members feel empowered to take risks, learn from their experiences, and develop their skills. By understanding that growth and development take time, perpetual encouragers foster a culture of learning, resilience, and personal growth within their teams.

Living in the shadow of the great Coach Nick Saban, I've learned that "*perfection is not achievable, but encouragement can help someone pursue it, and in that pursuit, they may just catch excellence.*" Leaders have a tremendous influence on the motivation and confidence of their team members. Discouraging someone from attempting something because they lack certain skills can lead to missed opportunities for growth and development.

Instead, leaders should adopt a more supportive approach by assessing the skills that are lacking and providing guidance on how to acquire them. By doing so, leaders can empower their team members to take on new challenges and develop the necessary skills to achieve their goals.

Coaching plays a crucial role in this process. Leaders should not only identify the missing skills but also provide resources, training, and mentorship to help individuals acquire those skills. This approach not only enables personal growth but also strengthens the overall skill set of the team.

Furthermore, leaders should encourage a culture of continuous learning and improvement. By fostering an environment where acquiring new skills is valued, leaders can inspire their team members to take initiative and pursue self-development. This mindset shift can lead to increased innovation, creativity, and overall team performance.

Leaders have the power to either discourage or empower their team members. By taking the time to assess missing skills and offering guidance on acquiring them, leaders can support individuals in achieving their goals and fostering a culture of growth and development. I find it extremely frustrating when leaders find it so easy to discourage others from attempting something because they don't initially or immediately have the skills needed. I call this the *Not Yet Syndrome*, which simply means that given time and opportunity, the person will acquire the skills they don't have YET! So, stick with them and encourage them to pursue it.

Most successful people have acquired the necessary skills over time. In my case, I have continually sought to grow as a leader, and have been able to continually add to my leadership toolbox. Perpetual encouragers recognize each person's enormous potential for growth, particularly when they lead with their head, their hands, their feet, their heart, and their mouth.

I am indebted to those who encouraged me through the years, and I'm happy for the opportunity to share this encouragement and its impact with others. If you want to be an empowering leader, then you must master the art of being a perpetual encourager.

Disclaimer: Being a perpetual encourager does not mean that you ignore the things in your organization that must be corrected. As a perpetual encourager, there are times when you've reached the end of your encouragement collateral and have to call a "Come to Jesus" meeting. But even in those intense and sometimes difficult circumstances, the goal is to correct the behavior to help (encourage) the team member be better, which, in turn, helps the organization. Perpetual encouragement is not the "We All Get a Trophy Mentality." Rather, it is the mindset you adopt by answering: "How do I make others better, and how do I be the best I can be?"

This is not a Christian book, but many of the principles that I have shared thus far have come directly from the Bible. So, I felt it necessary to dedicate a section to how the scriptures can help us deal with tough times and offer encouragement.

While scripture is replete with commands to encourage, encouragement does not always abound in our world. We often encounter people and attitudes that discourage us at work, at home, and even at church. Despite our best attempt, we can sometimes serve as the source of that discouragement for someone else.

There are many factors that can impact our ability to encourage or discourage people. However, for the sake of time and space, I'm only going to focus on a couple of key factors that impact our ability to be encouragers and the scriptures we can use to overcome them.

Factors that Impact Our Ability to Encourage

1) *Adults Suffering from a Wounded Spirit.* Many people are simply the wounded adult version of the child who was traumatized or hurt as they grew up in an environment filled with constant criticism, put-downs, and other forms of verbal abuse. They had their successes mocked and their accomplishments minimized. Rather than gaining positive self-esteem and feeling good about themselves, they questioned their own worth and value in the eyes of their families, friends, and even themselves.

These individuals often have a tough time receiving and accepting genuine encouragement and will initially require it in consistent yet small doses. They often perceive themselves as having very little self-worth and even lesser value to others. Fortunately, if you can help them identify their pain and wounds, and help them heal their wounded spirit, they will become one of the most effective encouragers on your team. They will use their new-found healing and encouragement to be a witness and encourager for those who may have suffered from the same feelings and treatment that set up camp in their hearts. God placed them in an enviable position in which they can say, "I was there. I understand!" Those 5 words may be the most consoling words a wounded soul may ever hear. It is important to note that some wounded people may require professional help that you can't offer, in which you can guide them, support them, and encourage them to seek professional help to heal their childhood wounds or trauma.

The words of the reckless pierce like swords, but the tongue of the wise brings healing. – Prov. 12:18

2) *We never learned how to encourage.* Knowledge is gained through teaching and observation. In certain families, humor is often used to embarrass members—particularly the younger ones. It usually isn't intended to be cruel, but often ends up having this effect. However, we are not educating our children to be encouragers in these circumstanccs.

We belittle them as a joke, but what we're really doing is marking them. One of my pet peeves is when a parent says, "You will never..." or "You always..." It's even worse when a parent calls a child stupid, dumb, slow, and so on! It doesn't seem important, but there is life or death in our words. So, when another adult, teacher, or fellow student uses the same words, it can take root and become real to the child. For our confidence and self-esteem to grow, we need to receive good comments from those closest to us, especially during our early years. This is not to say that misconduct is not corrected; quite the contrary, it must be corrected. However, it indicates that the person's sincere efforts and positive successes should be appreciated. Receiving such affirmation instills in us a desire to encourage others and assists in developing the insight and abilities necessary to do so.

"Fathers, do not exasperate your children; instead, bring (encourage) them up in the training and instruction of the Lord." - Eph 6:4

When we take the encouragement verses of scripture seriously, we can help build people up, guiding them to reach their maximum potential and their God-given destiny.

One of my favorite stories in the Bible comes from King David's life in the book of First Samuel. David had failed in the eyes of those he was called to lead.

Here is the story directly from the pages of the scriptures: *And it came to pass, when David and his men were come to Ziklag on the third day, that the Amalekites had invaded the south, and Ziklag, and smitten Ziklag, and burned it with fire; 2 And had taken the women captives, that were therein: they slew not any, either great or small, but carried them away, and went on their way. 3 So David and his men came to the city, and behold, it was burned with fire; and their wives, and their sons, and their daughters, were taken captives. 4 Then David and the people that were with him lifted their voice and wept, until they had no more power to weep. 5 And David's two wives were taken captives, Ahinoam the Jezreelitess, and Abigail the wife of Nabal the Carmelite.*

At this point in the story, we can empathize with David and his feelings, but most of us do not have the same response that he had, nor do we understand the nature of his response. But his response is one of the most important lessons that you and I can learn during our journey in becoming a perpetual encourager.

"And David was greatly distressed; for the people spake of stoning him, because the soul of all the people was grieved, every man for his sons and for his daughters: but David encouraged himself in the Lord his God."

- I Samuel 30:6

Despite being greatly distressed, being threatened with bodily harm, and having caused grief for every man he was leading, David chose to encourage himself in the Lord. The takeaway is this: *"When there is no one in your camp to encourage you, you need to be able to encourage yourself."*

Various factors work against our desire and ability to encourage others, but they can all be overcome by our commitment to encourage ourselves and others, as well as looking to the scriptures and other encouraging works to inspire our thoughts. When used correctly, the encouragement you find in scripture will revitalize both the encourager and the encouraged.

Chapter 19: How to Use Encouragement to Inspire Others

Each of us possesses a combination of positive and negative characteristics. Success comes to those who focus on the positive, minimize the negative, and work diligently to accomplish their goals. What better way to bring out the best qualities in others than to encourage and inspire them to pursue their endeavours?

Encouragement and inspiration are powerful tools that can help individuals unlock their full potential and overcome any obstacles they may face. By focusing on the positive aspects of someone's abilities and providing support, we can motivate them to strive for greatness and achieve their goals.

When we encourage others, we acknowledge their strengths and capabilities, boosting their confidence and self-belief. By highlighting their positive qualities, we help them recognize their own potential and encourage them to step out of their comfort zones. This can lead to increased motivation, determination, and a willingness to take on challenges that they may have otherwise avoided.

Inspiration is equally important in bringing out the best in others. Sharing stories of success, perseverance, and personal growth can ignite a spark within individuals, showing them what is possible and giving them a sense of direction. When someone sees others who have achieved greatness, they are inspired to follow in their footsteps and strive for their own success.

Moreover, encouragement and inspiration create a positive and supportive environment, fostering collaboration and teamwork. When individuals feel motivated and inspired, they are more likely to work together, share ideas, and support one another in reaching their collective goals. This sense of unity and cooperation can lead to even greater accomplishments and a more fulfilling journey towards success.

However, it is important to remember that bringing out the best in others is not a one-time effort. It requires ongoing support, guidance, and belief in their abilities. By consistently encouraging and inspiring others, we can help them stay focused, overcome setbacks, and continue to grow and develop. So, let us strive to be a source of motivation and support for those around us, empowering them to pursue their endeavors and achieve greatness.

Encouragement has the power and potential to motivate people to undertake things they would not have attempted otherwise. It motivates others to achieve their goals by demonstrating that you trust them even more than they trust themselves. It is a mandate of confidence. It contributes to the development of leaders and the strengthening of the organizational culture.

Encouragement builds team morale by inspiring, rousing, and motivating people with courage and optimism. It is a powerful instrument for interpersonal collaboration and cooperation. It boosts self-esteem and provides valuable feedback on what individuals are doing well and where they can improve. Encouragement enables us to make mistakes without dreading repercussions and allows us to lead to a better use of our resources.

As mentioned earlier, accepting encouragement is just as important as giving it, as it helps both the giver and the receiver. Accepting encouragement gracefully and with joy demonstrates to the person encouraging you that you value their opinion and perspective.

As with anything else, there can be drawbacks to excessive encouragement or giving it for unworthy behavior, especially in the case of children. They begin to cherish their work, not for its intrinsic value, but for the encouragement they will receive from others. So, they begin to work for the encouragement and not the work itself and when the encouragement is lacking, the quality of the work suffers.

Genuine encouragement comes from a place of sincerity and belief in the individual's abilities. It is not just empty words, but a true expression of support and belief in the person's potential. This type of encouragement can be a powerful motivator, helping the individual stay focused and determined in pursuit of their goals.

When encouragement is heartfelt, it can have a lasting impact on the individual's confidence and self-belief. It can inspire them to push through challenges and setbacks, knowing that they have someone who believes in them and their abilities. In contrast, insincere encouragement can often feel hollow and disingenuous, ultimately undermining the individual's motivation and drive.

Therefore, it is important to offer genuine encouragement to others, recognizing their efforts and achievements in a meaningful way. By doing so, we can help cultivate a positive and empowering environment that fosters growth and success for everyone involved.

Here are some recommendations for effectively employing encouragement.

1. Be candid and specific when reinforcing positive sentiments that indicate that the team member is liked and respected. Be sure to confirm that you accept and appreciate their activities and behavior.

2. Make an effort to focus on the positive actions people perform in their daily lives rather than their mistakes or failures.

3. Always be ready to step in when someone experiences a setback, failure, or disappointment because this is an optimal time to offer encouragement. This is also when the individual is most likely to receive and internalize your encouragement.

4. Demonstrate your genuine appreciation and concern by encouraging team members.

5. Encouragement should be delivered openly and not disguised as false praise.

When we develop the habit of observing others and providing encouragement when it is appropriate, we will notice a shift in both the people and the environment around us.

People will be more optimistic and will set out to achieve more than they previously believed was possible.

Scientific and psychological research has established the significant benefits of positive, verbal encouragement—particularly when it is constant—because it results in increased optimism.

Below are a few effective ways to communicate encouragement that maximizes its benefit to the recipient. However, if you make the effort, you will also experience the amazing rewards of being the provider of encouragement.

To begin, be sincere and intentional.

Randomly tossing kindness is good, but sharing your true, positive thoughts with someone helps you reach a higher level of healthy and encouraging communication. When you're sincere, you will look the person in the eye, and may even reach out to pat them on the back, squeeze their hand, or offer them a warm hug as appropriate.

Each of these contributes to the confirmation of the words spoken and enhances their effectiveness and authenticity. This helps distinguish the genuine encourager from the random, positive, verbal-joy-flingers. By the way, we appreciate the verbal-joy-flingers, but as leaders, we want to be perceived as sincere and intentional.

Perpetual encouragers are endowed with an inherent genuineness and optimism that we would all do well to emulate. Especially when it is that one-on-one, honest, and direct encouragement. It's worth it and only takes a moment to be kind to another person. Increase your intentional effort to connect with honesty.

Secondly, be precise.
Has anyone amazed, pleased, or inspired you lately?

Is it their vivacious smile? Is it their contrite apology? Is it their work ethic?

When encouraging someone, it's more effective and beneficial to specify what it is about them that makes you happy, and how they have inspired or impressed you. It's all too easy to think something nice about someone but miss the opportunity to let those words fly from your lips and dance in their ears. Deposit those words of encouragement at that very moment. Don't hold it; invest it!

You could simply say, "Rebecca, you have such an amazing smile," and that would almost certainly make her day. However, if you were more precise and stated, "Rebecca, you have the most beautiful smile. Each time I see it, it reminds me to smile more. It's contagious," your words would have a much larger impact.

Being precise in your encouragement requires only an additional breath but can ensure that the recipient never forgets how vital and precious their presence is to you and others. For each person to be reminded of their inherent worth simply by being themselves is immensely powerful, motivating, and encouraging.

Thirdly, be unpredictable.

By practicing encouragement, we can improve our ability to give it, and therefore increase the amount of positive energy that emanates from us, which, in turn, makes us more positive people and creates a more positive culture.

When you are real and precise, you can go about your normal day without skipping a beat, spreading the power of encouragement at every opportunity.

Practice telling your team members that their dedication and perseverance inspire you. Inform the barista at the coffee shop that their warm smile is appreciated. Take time to approach the gentleman who just assisted an elderly woman in opening a door and express your appreciation for his act of compassion. As you do this, you will find it much easier to spot people doing the right thing and find it easier for you to be an encourager.

I must emphasize that exercising genuine, specific, and spontaneous encouragement works well with most people, most of the time, but it is especially beneficial in our closest and more intertwined relationships. So, I encourage you to become spontaneous with those closest to you, especially family, friends, and members of your team. Sincere acts of kindness have the power to revitalize a relationship, re-establish trust, earn respect, and express love.

For example, if someone has been selfless enough to apologize or accept responsibility for any error, this is the ideal time to answer with, “I appreciate you saying that. That means a lot to me. Let’s see how we can learn from this and get better.” This reinforces the desire to focus on the positive aspects of the circumstance (the apology) and provides an opportunity for everyone to breathe in the healing power of humility and encouragement.

It’s also beneficial to explicitly express your gratitude: "I appreciate your assistance in preparing dinner. I understand you're exhausted, and I appreciate it.” Or try something like, “Thank you for bringing out the trash. You are such an asset to this team.” Practice finding different words to encourage sincerely, precisely, and spontaneously, and always consider the individual’s unique personality, background, and actions.

Do you make an effort to speak positively about others? Do you take note of their admirable characteristics and inform them of what you see? Do you use words of encouragement?

By delivering encouraging words, we build courage in others. Individuals who trust in themselves will give their all. By expressing encouraging words, we encourage others to continue in the positive direction they are headed or to take a course correcting action, if headed in the wrong direction.

When you offer words of encouragement, the positive energy they contain awakens their spirit. For instance, simply complimenting a waiter on his excellent service may make the waiter more receptive to you, and he will go out of his way to continue to satisfy you.

You may think the service is excellent, but that will benefit neither the waiter nor you if your thoughts remain unspoken. Encouragement is such a fundamental act, but we rarely do it automatically. When was the last time you expressed gratitude to your spouse, a friend, a relative, or a stranger? Do you require that people do exceptionally well to be worthy of your encouraging words or expressions? Do you simply take the opportunity to inspire others every chance you get?

Assist Others in Developing Their Potential

I am not advocating for praising substandard achievement, yet a few well-chosen words of encouragement can help improve substandard performance. To get the best that someone has to offer, we may have to help them find the gift(s) that lie within them.

This is not accomplished by attempting to change a person's nature, but by helping them discover and build upon the better qualities of who they are at their core. The goal is to encourage them to build on their existing talents. This type of encouragement is not natural because it goes against the human tendency to focus on the negative instead of the positive. Poet, Kahlil Gibran said, "Our greatest failing is our fixation on the faults of others."

Encourage Yourself

It is important that we encourage others, but it is even more important that we encourage ourselves. Others may not notice your progress or pay much attention to you and your efforts. They may not give your spirit the morale boost you so desperately need. So, it's important that if no one else believes in you or encourages you, you must establish a sense of self-confidence and strong faith in yourself. What you do not receive from others, you can obtain from your own inner strength. Never again should you solely depend on the compliment of another person to be encouraged. Circle back and read the story of King David at Ziklag for more insight into this principle.

Restoring Harmony

Encouragement can restore harmony or bring peace during turbulent times. In many of the books and movies we read and watch, we observe the destruction caused by mean-spirited, spiteful characters experiencing mental and physical breakdowns due to their thoughts and actions. The story usually ends with them having family and friends who encourage them to seek help, face their devils, and make the necessary changes and sacrifices to get or be better. As a result of the encouragement, they recognize the wrongs of their conduct, make amends, and restore equilibrium. Even though I used a hypothetical scenario, this translates perfectly into the real world. If you have a team member or family member that is struggling, then your encouragement can be the catalyst that lifts them out of their respective pit.

To right the ship and stay on course once they have started the journey to success, they must control and direct their thoughts towards positive transformation. The mind is like a wild horse; it will do as it pleases without a master to rein it in. There is an epidemic of people refusing to rein their mind in, and as my CEO likes to say, "People have lost civility." As a whole, we have let our brains wander uncontrollably with little regard for ourselves or the feelings and interests of others. If we're going to enjoy harmony and peace, we must deliberately seek to master our negative thoughts and behaviors and follow the encouragement we're given.

Be the Difference You Want to See: Smile at the Unfriendly

People tend to have a favorable view of those who attempt to mend broken connections. We can begin changing our lives at any point because we are the ones who possess the keys to the entanglements that we have created for ourselves. So, turn the key to the right in your life and begin the mending process.

Enhancing another person's potential will only add to the luster of your accomplishment. By recognizing others' efforts and boosting their self-esteem, you contribute to creating a better world or another way to say it is—you help others be more successful. In closing, if you complain that strangers no longer smile or are unfriendly, you can change the status quo by smiling first and be the change you want to see.

A bad atmosphere is the last thing you need when you're leading a team and need to convey a vital message. Not only will people not listen to you, but they will also seek something else to divert their attention away from you.

People do not necessarily do this on purpose, but they will do this because they're stuck in a toxic environment that perpetuates this kind of behavior. That is why it is important to create and maintain a positive atmosphere.

People surrounded by positive people generally feel energized when they hear genuine and authentic words of encouragement; there is such a beneficial effect on the environment that a simple word of encouragement can instantaneously remove the dark, heavy feeling associated with a negative culture.

What an incredible privilege! Possessing the ability to change the atmosphere is an incredible opportunity! And we are all capable of doing so. You do not need to be a leader to participate. You can do it even if you are the newest member of your team or younger than the individual you are conversing with!

For example, if you are a team leader, encourage your teammates before or during the meeting. Recognize them for their accomplishments from their previous performance or for helping grow the team. Whenever possible, solicit their input and feedback.

You don't necessarily have to encourage every squad member individually and can instead recognize the overall effort of the team and assist them in identifying their worth. If you succeed in doing so, I'm confident that the atmosphere in that meeting will be so positive that everyone will look forward to the next one.

That being said, it is important to understand the differences between having a positive or negative atmosphere in the workplace or in your personal life. The following outlines these differences.

POSITIVE ATMOSPHERE:

Excellent ambiance

Individuals grow more delighted to be a part of the team and begin to consider it a privilege rather than a duty. That is the ideal team. Individuals who volunteer to be a part of the team and are not persuaded or coerced to do so. This creates buy-in.

Individuals are empowered

Empowerment is among the most important values that a leader can impart to their team members. It is where true growth occurs. That's the point at which the mentality switches from the leader's obligation to the team member's responsibility.

You do not need to accomplish anything independently as a team leader! You've assembled an entire team that is eager and excited to contribute to something fantastic! And when the atmosphere is conducive to empowerment, individuals feel empowered! Individuals have been asked to and convinced they need to participate, and they step up to the plate and get it done.

Individuals can express themselves

Each individual brings something unique to the table. Since each of us are diverse and special, someone will have a skill that others don't. That is why it is important to know who those individuals are, and to understand what each team member has to offer.

However, it will be extremely difficult to achieve this if your team members do not feel they can be open and feel stifled by your leadership style. You're unlikely to elicit anything from them if they feel this way. However, when they feel the security provided by a positive atmosphere, they will be willing to share their most intimate thoughts and creative ideas, which you can then use to better the team's overall performance and cooperation.

A positive atmosphere alleviates the tension created by negativity and the expectation that the person in charge will criticize you if you speak up. As someone who wishes to have people open up, we must learn to encourage them and recognize their gifts and enthusiasm.

NEGATIVE ATMOSPHERE:
Individuals are incapable of rational thought

When the atmosphere is heavy and negative, people's minds become muddled. Even someone intelligent and creative will find it quite difficult to function successfully in this environment. If you're leading in a negative environment, you are unlikely to persuade team members to share openly and honestly.

Individuals will begin to think negatively

Always avoid negativity. There is nothing positive to be gained from it. It suffocates the overall vision, enthusiasm, and joy. What negativity produces is fairly predictable behavior that generally doesn't deviate from the expected patterns. Negativity has a profound effect on people and keeps them from progressing as expected. It usually keeps them stagnant for an extended period. By simply being aware of the effect of negativity, we can eliminate or minimize its impact.

Individuals will not participate, even if they believe they have an excellent proposal

People desire to be a part of something greater and bigger than themselves. They desire to be a part of something enjoyable. They enjoy the exchanging of ideas and the team collaboration, especially when it serves to energize others. However, if the climate is toxic, innovative ideas will be scarce and those willing to offer them will be much fewer.

In a positive and supportive workplace, people are more productive, more focused, and more successful than those in negative workplaces. Our attitude and the proper use of encouragement are two of the biggest contributors to the development of that positive and supportive workplace.

Being encouraging and recognizing others is not only the correct thing to do, but it is also our obligation and privilege as leaders.

I believe employing encouraging language allows us to put our good intentions forward, supporting people into action. The following are examples of encouraging language. As with any other speech pattern, as you use and learn it, you will improve your fluency, confidence, and ability to use it more frequently and efficiently.

"I believe in you and have faith in your ability to get it done." Few words are as potent as these. When individuals learn that others believe in them, their self-esteem and self-confidence improves.

"I've been watching you and I really admire the way you handled that situation." When you offer encouragement in the form of praise, you are setting them up for success.

"I want you to know that you are loved and appreciated." "Thank you, I appreciate you." These two quotes represent one of the first things our parents hope we learn: to have an attitude of gratitude and show appreciation to others. It is more than a matter of courtesy. It communicates to others that we took notice of them and what they do.

"We need you/your assistance." Everyone wants to be needed. Invite your team members to join you in the journey, and always make them feel valuable and irreplaceable.

"What are your thoughts?" Inquiring about someone's input and ideas is an excellent method to demonstrate your appreciation for them.

"I'm confident you can do it." This is another approach to verbally expressing your convictions. I'm sure you can

recall a time when someone said it to you, and it changed your performance level (and maybe your life).

"How can I assist?" Our time is limited. It is extremely encouraging when we are willing to freely give it to others.

"I'll be there for you. You can count on me." Individuals do not wish to be alone. When we are willing to walk alongside others, they feel less fearful of future's unknowns and feel supported by you.

"What or how much do you need?" We all require something, and when someone inquires about what it is, it is extremely gratifying and shows that they empathize with us.

"I understand what you're saying." Empathy is a potent motivator. We do not have to allow someone to wallow in their problems; often, by hearing and empathizing with their condition, we can assist them in moving forward.

"I have faith in you." We are motivated to uphold that trust when we are trusted.

"Can you please explain further?" This evocative statement demonstrates our curiosity and readiness to listen. It makes the team member feel that their opinion matters.

As we encourage others, we create a more positive environment for ourselves. Even if your motivation for encouraging others is entirely selfish, you and your heart will benefit from your efforts, and the encouragement you offer will eventually become selfless. So, use the encouragement language throughout your journey toward becoming a perpetual encourager.

How often do you encourage others or receive encouragement?

I have been blessed with being a natural encourager, so I find it pretty easy to offer encouragement in everything I do. But when I choose to be more intentional about it, the impact of my encouragement is much more powerful for my team member. My ultimate goal is that even though I'm doing it intentionally, it doesn't come across as forced or fake. Since some of us are unaccustomed to or find it difficult to give and/or receive encouragement, we must work at it until it becomes natural. Practice is the only way to acquire this much needed skill. If it comes naturally, then you can focus on becoming a perpetual encourager and helping others do the same.

Consider the last time you were encouraged at work. Apart from a yearly assessment detailing your accomplishments and shortcomings, when was the last time you received a verbal pat on the back? Wouldn't you feel better about yourself and be more motivated to work if you felt appreciated?

On the other hand, when was the last time you acknowledged someone else's efforts? Perhaps, if you begin to speak encouraging words, others will follow suit. Let's look at some approaches that might be employed to motivate coworkers.

The following are examples of approaches that I have observed and used to encourage others through the years. Apply them and you will benefit from their positive impact and effectiveness.

1. When introducing someone, use a few words praising the individual's abilities and/or accomplishments.

2. Create a unique note for someone that includes examples of things you've spotted them doing well or improving on.

3. Incorporate celebration into your relationships on a regular basis. For instance, you may commemorate both

huge and minor wins by gathering for coffee or lunch, or you can do something as simple as a phone call or a high-five.

4. Be specific in your praise by providing an example. By doing so, you lend your encouragement greater credibility.

5. If someone in the workplace is working on a large project, send them something modest to demonstrate your concern and confidence in their capacity to perform an excellent job. For instance, if you know they enjoy chocolate, you could purchase a little box of chocolates for them.

6. Demonstrate real interest and demonstrate that you care about them as a person.

7. Recognize their priorities. After spending time with this person, you will begin to understand their concerns and interests and ask them questions about them.

8. Find a way to say, "Well done" or "Great work" before the project ends because sometimes, a word of

encouragement at the perfect time might be the difference between them quitting and persevering to the end.

9. Express gratitude. A simple thank you communicates to others that their efforts have been seen and appreciated.

10. Return the favor. If you appreciate anything someone does, a fantastic way to express your thanks is to return the favor.

11. Finally, and perhaps most gratifyingly, if you witness someone performing an outstanding job, send a note of congratulations to their supervisor/employer informing them of the worker's dedication.

Once you've implemented a few of these approaches, expressing encouragement will become more natural. You're much more likely to derive pleasure from making others feel valued.

The more you practice, the better you will get, and it will spark a positive atmosphere in your workplace. Sooner rather than later, you will feel confident in offering encouraging words, and before you know it, you will be a perpetual encourager.

I would like to share one more challenge to you when it comes to applying the content of this book and beginning your journey to becoming a perpetual encourager. In the first 9 versus of Joshua, he is initially encouraged and eventually commanded to be "strong and courageous." If a leader of the caliber of Joshua had to be encouraged to take his role as the leader of the nation of Israel, then we all need encouragement. Joshua had been one of the 12 spies sent in to spy on the Promised Land. Even though 10 of the spies and the entire nation of Israel were afraid to enter the Promised Land, Joshua stated, "Despite the giants, with God they were well able to take the land" (paraphrased). I point this out because the need for encouragement can be situational and we must all be ready to step in and offer it, as well as receive it. So, I'm encouraging you to be "strong and courageous" and face your future with the confidence and boldness of a champion.

To close this labor of love, I would like to remind you that as humans, we all tend to keep a little in reserve and not give 100% without some type of outside influence. This is where coaching/encouragement comes into the picture.

Please resume the following position: Please sit down and raise both your hands as high as you can. This challenge demonstrates the power of encouragement and how it can maximize the leadership potential of others.

Raise Your Hand Challenge:

1. Raise both your hands **as high as you can** and hold them up for 3-5 seconds.
2. Now, give me **one more inch**. That's it! Stretch as far as you can. Did you get one more inch?
3. Now, most of you think you're at your max, but if you're seated, stand up and repeat steps 1-2.
4. Now, give me more! How? Stand on your tippy toes.
5. Yes, there can be even more. Stand on a chair, a table, a ladder, or anything around you that can hold your weight. Be careful!

Most people think that they've accomplished the goal at step one, but we all tend to hold back until someone comes along and asks us to give **one more inch**! I challenge you to incorporate the principles in this book into your leadership toolbox and help those you lead, give **one more inch.**

Please refer to these quotes to further fuel your encouragement, and to propel you further on your journey toward being a perpetual encourager.

"By encouraging others (by providing an incentive to act), you will gain courage and be encouraged." - W.C. Stone

"No such thing as a self-made' man exists. We are comprised of thousands of other individuals. Every person who has ever done us a favor or uttered a word of encouragement has contributed to the formation of our character and thoughts and our success." - Unknown

"Most people are not complacent, but they do feel a sense of inadequacy and often become frustrated with themselves; consequently, encouragement is important! I do it often! I congratulate everyone on anything they do that I believe is admirable." - Berg, David Brandt

"And we know that for those who love God all things work together for good, for those who are called according to His purpose." - Apostle Paul

"I can do all things through him who strengthens me." - Philippians 4:13

"Therefore, encourage one another and build one another up, just as you are doing." - I Thess 5:11

"I have said these things to you, that in me you may have peace. In the world you will have tribulation. But take heart; I have overcome the world." - John 16:33

"Have I not commanded you? Be strong and courageous. Do not be frightened, and do not be dismayed, for the Lord your God is with you wherever you go." - Joshua 1:9

"And let us consider how to stir up one another to love and good works, not neglecting to meet together, as is the habit of some, but encouraging one another, and all the more as you see the Day drawing near." - Hebrews 10:24-25

"Let no corrupting talk come out of your mouths, but only such as is good for building up, as fits the occasion, that it may give grace to those who hear." - Ephesians 4:29

"Despite your current circumstances—keep blocking—greatness awaits, but it waits for no one." - Martin Houston

"Your ability to succeed will be empowered by your ability to focus and keep the main things, the main things" – Martin Houston

"If you want to be successful, create a culture where others feel valued" – Martin Houston

"Your words can help others find that ***one more inch!****"* – Martin Houston

To contact or follow Martin:

Email: *martin@martinhouston.org* Website:

www.martinhoustonspeaks.org

The M-powerment Institute:

www. m-powermentinstitute.com

The Empowerment Center:

www.empowermentcenter.net

Social Media:

Facebook: *@themartinhouston35*

Twitter: *@martinhouston35*

Instagram: *@martinhouston35*

TikTok: *@martinhouston35*

Harvest Church: *www.hctuscaloosa.com*

Mail: The Link - 6110 Watermelon Rd, Northport, AL 35475

Made in the USA
Middletown, DE
09 September 2024